REASON TO WRITE

Student Handbook

Also by Douglas B. Reeves, Ph.D.

REASON TO WRITE:
Help Your Child Succeed in School and in Life Through Better Reasoning
and Clear Communication, Elementary School Edition

CRUSADE IN THE CLASSROOM:
How George W. Bush's Education Reforms Will Affect Your Children, Our Schools

20-MINUTE LEARNING CONNECTION:
A Practical Guide for Parents Who Want to Help Their Children Succeed in School,
Elementary School Edition

Available for the following states:

- · California
- · Florida
- · Illinois
- · Massachusetts
- · New York
- · Texas

20-MINUTE LEARNING CONNECTION:
A Practical Guide for Parents Who Want to Help Their Children Succeed in School,
Middle School Edition

Available for the following states:

- · California
- · Florida
- · Illinois
- · Massachusetts
- · New York
- · Texas

Douglas B. Reeves, Ph.D.

REASON TO WRITE

Student Handbook

Elementary School Edition

Kaplan Publishing

New York • London • Toronto • Sydney • Singapore

Kaplan Publishing
Published by Simon & Schuster, Inc.
1230 Avenue of the Americas
New York, NY 10020

For bulk sales to schools, colleges, and universities, please contact: Order Department, Simon & Schuster, Inc., 100 Front Street, Riverside, NJ 08075. Phone: (800) 223-2336. Fax: (800) 943-9831.

For information regarding special discounts for other bulk purchases, please contact Simon & Schuster Special Sales at 1-800-456-6798 or business@simonandschuster.com

Designed by Lisa Stokes

Manufactured in the United States of America

September 2002
10 9 8 7 6 5 4 3 2 1

Library of Congress Cataloging-in-Publication Data

ISBN: 0-7432-3053-1

The publisher wishes to thank Kayleigh Blanchette for her contribution to this book.

Contents

Introduction
Where Do I Start?

THIS book will help you become a better writer. You already have a great imagination and lots of ideas. Now you can use those ideas to write stories, essays,
letters, and poems. Each chapter has some important information that will help
you build your writing skills. In the beginning, we'll talk about why writing is
important. We'll also talk about the rules of good writing, and you'll create your
own personal set of rules. Then we'll talk about different kinds of writing, including letters, essays, stories, poems, research papers, and journal writing. At first,
you'll do only a little writing. I'll ask you some questions, and you'll write your
answers in this book. Later, you'll do more writing. By the time you have completed all of the worksheets in this book, you will be able to complete any writing assignment in any subject, including English, social studies, and science. Best
of all, you will be ready to enter middle school as a confident writer.

If you are already an experienced writer and need to work on a project right
now, you can jump straight to the chapters that have the information you need.

If you need help on descriptive writing, jump to chapter 11.
If you need help on analytical writing, jump to chapter 12.
If you need help on persuasive writing, jump to chapter 13.
If you need help on a research paper, jump to chapter 14.
If you need help on creative writing, jump to chapter 15.
If you need to practice essays for state tests, jump to chapter 17.

Let's get started!

1 Why Is Writing So Important?

WE haven't met yet, but I think I already know some important things about you. You like school, at least most of the time. You've been going to school long enough now to know that some days are better than other days. Some days are exciting, and others are boring. Most kids are nice, but some are mean. Most teachers care about you, but a few seem to be pretty stressed out. In other words, you're a pretty typical kid in a pretty typical school.

Now that I know a little about you, let me tell you a few things about me. My name is Doug, and I write books for teachers, parents, and kids. I have four children. Their names are Brooks, Alex, Julia, and James, and they are now in elementary school, middle school, high school, and college. I'm also a teacher, and have taught students in elementary school, middle school, high school, and college. And just like you, I'm also a student, because I'm always learning new things. Even though I'm a grown-up with kids and a job, I still go to school, take classes, and try to learn new things all the time. I am also taking cello lessons. I'm just a beginner, and I'm not very good at it yet, but I know that if I keep practicing, I'll get better. In fact, some of the things I've learned from being a student help me understand what you are going through in school. Sometimes being a student is fun, but sometimes it's frustrating. Sometimes my teacher says, "Good job!" and he really means it, and sometimes he says, "Good job," and I can tell that I still need a lot of work.

Even though we haven't met, I think I know a lot about how you feel about school and about writing. We both like to do our very best work. The problem is figuring out how to do that. This book will help you do your very best work in writing.

Thinking about your strengths and the things you care about most will help you be a better writer. So right now, please write down some important information about yourself in the box below.

My name: _____

In school, my three best subjects are:

_____

_____

_____

Things I do very well (try to think of different things than the subjects you listed above):

_____

_____

_____

I care very much about these three things:

_____

_____

_____

These three things make me mad:

_____

_____

_____

✐ WRITING FOR REAL PEOPLE

"But writing is easy!" you might say. "Every kid knows how to write!" There is a very important difference between writing words on a piece of paper and writing stories, essays, letters, and poems that make your ideas clear. Think about it this way. What do you need when you want to talk about something you care about or something that makes you mad? You need a listener. It's okay to talk in the bathtub or when you play with stuffed animals, but let's face it: It's much nicer when a real person is listening to you. Real people ask you questions. Real people want to learn more about your ideas. Real people show that they care about what you say. When you talk to a good listener, you want to tell your best stories and share your best ideas. When you imagine a reader for your writing, you will want to write your best so that your reader understands your ideas.

Think about who you like to share your ideas and stories with: a parent, a friend, or a teacher. Think about sharing your ideas with someone you've never met: a favorite author, an athlete you admire, or even someone you've read about in social studies or science class. Imagine these people as your readers. In the box below, list as many people as you can think about who might be interested in your writing.

MY AUDIENCE

Family:

_____

_____

_____

Relatives:

_____

_____

_____

Friends:

_____

_____

_____

Neighbors:

_____

_____

_____

Teachers:

_____

_____

_____

Other people who might want to read my writing:

_____

_____

_____

Each time you write, think of your reader. You are writing not only for yourself, but also for your audience.

WHY IS WRITING SO IMPORTANT?

You're probably pretty busy. Students like you are often involved in sports, after-school activities, playing with friends, music lessons, and lots of other things. You might think that writing takes too much time. Let me explain why writing is so important. Writing helps you in every subject in school. Writing helps you in reading, math, science, social studies, and anything that requires thinking.

When you read something that is hard to understand, writing a summary is a great way to help you remember what you have read. Your summary doesn't have to be fancy—just a few lines that help you recall the main idea and two or three details that support the main idea. Try it out on the passage below. Don't worry if terms like *trophic levels, tertiary consumers,* and *decomposers* are new to you. We're not going to read definitions, but we will learn about these words by reading about them.

Read the material in the text and then answer the questions. You will be surprised how much you understand even though it concerns a difficult subject with unusual words:

In the natural world, plants and animals need each other to survive. The food web helps us understand how plants and animals survive. There are different layers in the food web, and these are known as trophic levels. On each trophic level, there are different types of plants or animals. Decomposers are very tiny organisms that feed on dead plants and animals and break them down in the soil. This gives the earth the nutrients it needs to help plants grow. These plants are called producers.

Primary consumers are animals that eat plants. For example, grasshoppers and caterpillars are primary consumers. Secondary consumers are animals that eat plant-eating animals. Birds are secondary consumers. Tertiary consumers are animals that eat other meat-eating animals.

Questions

1. Describe one example of how plants and animals need each other.

_____

_____

2. What do you think would happen if there were no decomposers?

_____

_____

---

3. What do secondary consumers need to eat?

_____

Vocabulary Check

1. "Trophic levels" are layers in a _____.

2. "Tertiary consumers" are animals that eat other _____ animals.

3. "Decomposers" feed on _____.

Wow! You were great! I'll bet that you're the only one in your family who knows what a trophic layer is. Let's think about what just happened. You read a short paragraph with hard words and complicated information. You stopped, thought about it, wrote the answers to some questions, and then double-checked your understanding. In a very short time, you learned a lot of new information. Now think about what might have happened if you had tried to read ten pages of this kind of information. How would you feel? Probably you would be discouraged and maybe even a little angry. You might even ask, "How does the teacher expect me to know all this stuff?"

Think about what might have happened if we had started this chapter with the words, WARNING: TROPHIC LAYERS AND TERTIARY CONSUMERS AHEAD—ENTER AT YOUR OWN RISK! Many readers—maybe even you—would have said, "This book isn't for me. I don't know about those things, and I'm not sure that I want to know about them." In school, we don't always get to choose what we read. When we write about what we read, we understand it better. Even if your teacher doesn't ask you to write a summary of what you read, it's a great idea. This is especially important if the things you are reading are difficult or unusual. You don't need a checklist or a set of questions. Just make a few notes about the main idea and supporting details, list the words that are new, and write what you think those words mean.

One of the most important keys to good writing is good reading. One of the keys to good reading is the ability to write a summary about what you have read. It's a cycle—similar to the cycle in nature we just read about—in which reading and writing work together. You must be a good reader to be a good writer, and you need to be a good writer to be a better reader.

Now, let's go back to your list of "Things I Do Very Well" on page 2. You are ready to add these words:

I can read and understand complicated words.
I can summarize complicated ideas.
I can understand information that is brand-new and that I had never learned before.

2 What to Do If You Hate Writing

(And even if you don't hate writing, read this chapter anyway!)

SAM and Claudia hate writing. Sam thinks writing is boring. Claudia thinks she's no good at it. But you know something funny? Sam and Claudia are both great at doing other things. Sam is a great musician. He can sing, and he plays the piano so well that the music teacher, Ms. Liebowitz, lets him play for the school chorus. Claudia is the best soccer player in the whole school. It doesn't make any difference if she's playing with the girls or the boys, she is the top scorer in almost every game. How do you think Sam got to be such a good musician and Claudia got to be such a good soccer player? Write your ideas down here:

Sam is really good in music because:

_____

_____

_____

_____

_____

Claudia is really good in soccer because:

_____

_____

_____

_____

Now let's think about how other people help Sam and Claudia and how they help themselves.

When Claudia scores a goal in soccer and her Mom or Dad is watching, they say, "_____."

After Sam finishes playing the piano, he gets up and bows to the audience. When he does this, the audience _____

When Sam first looks at a piece of music, he can't play all of the notes right away. He has to take the music home and _____.

If you asked Claudia why playing soccer is so much fun, she might say, "_____ _____,"

If you asked Sam why he enjoys playing the piano, he might say, "_____ _____ ."

When Sam makes a mistake on the piano, what does he do?_____ _____ .

When Claudia misses a soccer goal during practice, what does she do? _____ _____ .

Sam knows that to be a good piano player, he has to _____ _____ .

Claudia knows that to be a good soccer player she has to _____

_____ .

Let's think about what we have learned about Sam and Claudia and see if it will help us give them advice about how to be better writers. In the areas where they are very, very good, Sam and Claudia work hard. Sam practices the piano, and Claudia kicks the soccer ball. People cheer when Claudia makes a goal, and they clap when Sam plays the piano. At first, Sam and Claudia were not very good in music and soccer, but the more they practiced, the better they got. Claudia likes soccer because she likes scoring goals, helping her team, and hearing people cheer for her. She likes to do things that she does well. Sam really doesn't like practicing the piano very much, but he really likes playing for the school chorus and loves hearing people applaud. Even when he doesn't know the music, he is willing to work hard at it and practice after school because he enjoys playing the piano well. Claudia and Sam still make some mistakes, but these mistakes don't bother them very much. They just try again and work harder until they get it right.

WHAT DO WE DO NOW?

We have a problem: Sam and Claudia still hate writing. Unfortunately, they have to do a lot of writing in school. They have to write book reports, science reports, social studies reports, and essays. They have to write letters, instructions, and stories. "It's easy for some kids," Sam says, "but not for me." "That's right," adds Claudia. "Every time I try to do an essay, it just comes out wrong. My teacher makes red marks, my parents get mad, and even some of my friends giggle. It's awful!"

Sam and Claudia are frustrated and unhappy, and they have come to you for advice. Before you give advice to Sam and Claudia, think about the other people involved in their success in school. First, give advice to their parents. Then give advice to their teachers and friends. Finally, give some advice to Sam and Claudia.

My Advice to the Parents of Sam and Claudia

If you want Sam and Claudia to enjoy writing as much as they enjoy music and soccer, then you should:

_____

_____

_____

_____

My Advice to the Teacher

If you want Sam and Claudia to work as hard at writing as they do at music and soccer, then you should:

_____

_____

_____

_____

My Advice to the Friends of Sam and Claudia

If you want to help Sam and Claudia to be as good at writing as they are at music and soccer, then you should:

_____

_____

_____

_____

_____

My Advice to Sam and Claudia

Sam, you are a great piano player, and you enjoy it. Claudia, you are the best soccer player in the school, and you enjoy playing soccer more than just about anything. But you both say that you hate writing. You probably won't be very good at something that you hate. I've been thinking about some lessons that you can learn from music and soccer and how they might help you enjoy writing a lot more. If you want to enjoy writing and become good at it, then you should:

_____

_____

_____

_____

_____

BUILDING ON YOUR STRENGTHS

You may not hate writing as much as Sam and Claudia do, but you probably have some areas where you are strong and other areas where you are not so strong. Not being good at something can make us feel worried and upset. But the best way to get better at something is to think about things we do really well.

How did you help Sam and Claudia? You used what you learned about their strengths in music and soccer to give advice to Sam and Claudia and to their parents, teachers, and friends. What about you? What are your strengths? How did you become as good in your area of strength as Claudia is in soccer and as Sam is in music?

My Strengths: Reasons for My Strengths:

_____   _____

                                       _____

                                       _____

_____   _____

                                       _____

                                       _____

_____   _____

                                       _____

                                       _____

You are going to become a better writer by building on your strengths.

3 What You Really Need to Know for School

THIS chapter is about the kinds of writing you need to be able to do for school. Your school may not make you do all of these things, but here is one thing that I can promise you: If you are able to do the things listed in this chapter by the time you leave elementary school, you will be a great student in middle school or junior high school.

Before you leave elementary school, this is what you need to be able to do:

write a research paper, including a bibliography;
write a persuasive essay, supported by evidence;
write an analytical essay in literature, science, social studies, and the arts;
write a descriptive essay, using details and imagery;
write creatively, including short stories and poems;
write legibly by hand and use a word processor;
write using the conventions of English grammar, punctuation, and spelling.

That's a lot! It may be a lot more than you are doing now. If you are not doing all of these things in your school, it is probably because your teachers are very busy with many other things. But when you go to middle school or junior high school, you will still be expected to know all of these types of writing, even if you didn't have time to work on them in elementary school. That is why it is so important for you to spend some time on writing at home.

Using the following chart in Figure 3.1, rate yourself in one of four categories:

4—I'm so good at this, I could teach the class!

3—I'm pretty good at this, but I wouldn't want to try to help anyone else.

2—I know what this is, but I can't do it as well as I need to yet.

1—I really don't know what this is.

You may know how to do many of these things. You may be so good at some things that you could help other students. That's great! You will also find some things that you know about, but where you need some more time and practice. And you will probably find some things that you just haven't heard about yet.

When you have completed this form, talk to your parents and your teacher. The first question to ask is, "Do you agree with my ratings of myself?" Once you have listened to their ideas about your strengths, then you might want to offer to help other students in those areas where you are a 4. You can also ask for some help in those areas where you are a 1 or 2.

The numbers in the parentheses in the first column tell you the grade when each writing skill is usually taught. For example, (5) means that most schools won't ask students do this type of writing until the fifth grade. Your school may be different. So no matter what grade you are in now, fill out the entire form. Find those things you do well and find some where you need some work. This will help you understand your strengths and also help you, your parents, and your teacher work on areas where you need some more time.

Writing Skill (Grade)	4 — I know this so well that I can teach it to other students.	3 — I know this well, but am not ready to teach someone else.	2 — I know about this, but I need to work on it a little more.	1 – I haven't heard of this and can't do it right now.	Teacher/Parent Comments
Write brief story describing an experience (1).					
Write in complete sentences (1).					
Retell stories, including who, what, where, when, how, and why (1).					
Print legibly (1).					
Use a simple web to plan my writing (2).					

Figure 3.1. Rate Your Writing Skills

Writing Skill (Grade)	4 — I know this so well that I can teach it to other students.	3 — I know this well, but am not ready to teach someone else.	2 — I know about this, but I need to work on it a little more.	1 – I haven't heard of this and can't do it right now.	Teacher/Parent Comments
Write a paragraph with a topic sentence and supporting details (2).					
Write an outline (3).					
Write a first draft, then edit, revise, and create a final draft (3).					
Edit the work of other students, making suggestions and finding mistakes (3).					
Write descriptive pieces about people, places, things, or events (3).					

Writing Skill (Grade)	4 — I know this so well that I can teach it to other students.	3 — I know this well, but am not ready to teach someone else.	2 — I know about this, but I need to work on it a little more.	1 – I haven't heard of this and can't do it right now.	Teacher/Parent Comments
Use periods, exclamation points, and question marks at the end of sentences (3).					
Write legibly in cursive (3).					
Write three or more paragraphs, with an introductory paragraph (4).					
Use correct indentation of paragraphs (4).					
Write a formal letter (4).					

Writing Skill (Grade)	4 — I know this so well that I can teach it to other students.	3 — I know this well, but am not ready to teach someone else.	2 — I know about this, but I need to work on it a little more.	1 – I haven't heard of this and can't do it right now.	Teacher/Parent Comments
Write a persuasive essay with examples or evidence to support your point of view (4).					
Write a summary of text (about four hundred words) that is accurate and in order (4).					
Use a word processor to create a document, save it, and print it (4).					
Write an informational essay with five or more paragraphs (5).					
Write sentences that make transitions from one paragraph to the next (5).					

Writing Skill (Grade)	4 — I know this so well that I can teach it to other students.	3 — I know this well, but am not ready to teach someone else.	2 — I know about this, but I need to work on it a little more.	1 – I haven't heard of this and can't do it right now.	Teacher/Parent Comments
Write a research report about important ideas, issues, or events (5).					
Give credit to other writers if I use their words. (5).					
Include a chart, table, or graph in a paper in both a word processor and handwritten document (5).					

Summary of my strengths as a writer:

_____

_____

_____

_____

The areas of writing where I am best are:

_____

_____

_____

_____

The areas of writing where I need some more time are:

_____

_____

_____

_____

4
You're Smarter Than You Think: What You Already Know About Good Writing

GOOD writers take ordinary events and make them seem special. Let's think about something we all experience every day, the weather. Here are two ways of describing the weather on a rainy night:

CINDY: "It rained last night. It rained a lot. The thunder was loud. The lightning scared me when it was so bright."

KATE: "My eyes opened when I heard the first drops of water hit the window by my bed. Soon, the drops became louder, pouring buckets of water from the sky. Then the rumble of thunder grew louder until it crashed outside my window, shaking the glass. Soon I was shaking too, afraid that the glass would break and I would be alone in the middle of the storm. A few seconds later, lightning flashed so bright that I could see the outline of our neighbor's house. Within minutes, the thunder had passed and there was only the soft sound of raindrops on my window."

Both writers heard the same rainstorm. Which description did you like better? Why?

I prefer the description by _____ because:
_____
_____
_____

WHAT YOU ALREADY KNOW ABOUT GOOD WRITING

Let's think about what you already know about good writing. You already know that details are important. You know that exciting words help writers communicate better and that words do not have to be big or unfamiliar to be exciting. For example, Kate used words such as *rumble* and *flash* to describe the thunder and lightning. You know that writing is more interesting when the sentences begin differently. Cindy's sentences all seem to be alike, but each sentence in Kate's paragraph starts a little bit differently. You also know that good writing can appear in unexpected places. Although some readers expect exciting events to happen only in stories about imaginary characters, Kate was able to make the opening paragraph of her science essay about weather sound very exciting.

YOUR PERSONAL RULES FOR GOOD WRITING

Almost every teacher and classroom has rules. Most of these rules have to do with times to be quiet, respecting other people and property, and littering. Class rules are usually very clear so that everybody knows what they mean. Even a new kid in school can quickly learn the rules and stay out of trouble. Think about your classroom rules and how you would explain them to a new student in your class. List them in the box on page 24.

Our Classroom Rules

_____

_____

_____

_____

Think about the list you just created. I'll bet your rules are more than just "sit still and be quiet." Is there a rule about respecting other people or about keeping the classroom neat? Thinking about class rules reminds us that there is more to a successful classroom than quiet students.

Now let's create some rules for writing that are as clear as your classroom rules. Imagine that you are explaining your personal rules for good writing to a new student in your class. Try to make your list of rules specific and complete.

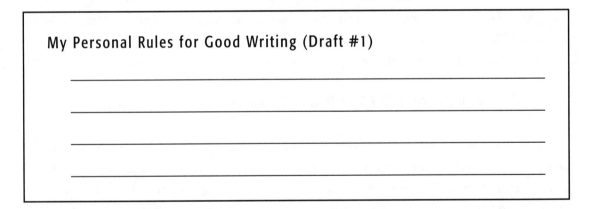

My Personal Rules for Good Writing (Draft #1)

_____

_____

_____

_____

If you are like most students, your personal rules for good writing include writing neatly, putting your name on the paper, and spelling words correctly. Those are all very important things, and I'm glad that you put them in your personal rules for good writing. As we continue in this workbook, you will find some other things that are also very important for good writing. You'll learn about these rules by reading examples of good writing and thinking about what makes them good. For example, Kate helped us learn that good writers use details and exciting words. Kate's paragraph also showed us that an exciting introduction can help grab the reader's attention, even if the topic is not one that we thought was very interesting at first.

When you think about other qualities of good writing, what else can you think of? Just as we know that a good set of classroom rules includes more than "sit still and be quiet," a good set of rules for writers must cover more than spelling, grammar, and punctuation. We know that interesting details and ideas are important. We also know that organization is helpful, so that your writing has a clear beginning, middle, and end. Word choice is also an important part of good writing. Do you remember how Kate's words made the thunder and lightning seem to shake the room as you were reading? When you write, it is important to choose the best words to tell the reader exactly what you mean. And, just in case you forgot to list it in your first draft, the rules of punctuation, spelling, and grammar really are important. When you follow the rules of punctuation, spelling, and grammar, it is easier for the reader to understand your meaning. Think about these things and any other ideas that you want to add. Now create your second draft of "My Personal Rules for Writing."

My Personal Rules for Good Writing (Draft #2)

_____

_____

_____

_____

Now, compare your rules for good writing to your rules for classroom behavior. Could you explain to another student how to write well, just as you could explain to a new kid in class what the classroom rules are? As we learn more in the rest of this book, you will be able to revise and add to your personal rules for good writing. By the end of this book, you won't need my rules, your teacher's rules, or anyone else's rules for good writing. You'll have your own rules for good writing.

Sometimes my son who is in third grade, Jamie, likes to say, "I'm in charge!" He likes saying it because there are not very many times in the life of a third grader when he gets to be in charge, especially when he has a sister in seventh grade and a brother in ninth grade. Jamie does get to be in charge when he sets his own rules for writing, and now, you are in charge, too. If you would like, make a copy of your second draft of "My Personal Rules for Good Writing" and put it in your notebook or write your rules on a poster and display them in your bedroom or wherever you do your homework. It will help you remember the things that are most important and, as we continue in this book, you will think of new things to add to your list.

5 The Audience

IN chapter 2, you gave some advice to Sam and Claudia's parents about how to help their children become better writers. What did you say? I wouldn't be surprised if you wrote something like this: "If you want your kids to be better writers, you ought to cheer just as hard for their writing as you do when they score a goal in soccer or play the piano well."

Parents, teachers, and friends are all very important members of your audience when you play sports or music. The audience cheers when you do well and offers encouragement when you try hard. The audience pays attention and wants you to do your very best.

The same is true of writing. Your audience pays attention and wants you to do your very best. The audience is your partner.

You may have many different kinds of audiences when you write. Different audiences have different interests. Try to imagine an audience when you write. When you write about your family, your grandparents would be a good audience. When you write about the rain forest, your friends who are interested in nature would be a great audience. When you write about sports, your coach and your teammates might be good audience members. Think of it this way: When you speak, you want the other person to really listen. You want to speak with someone who is interested in what you have to say. You also want to speak clearly and explain your ideas so your listener understands them. When you write, you want the reader to pay attention. You also want to write so that your reader understands your ideas.

When you think about the people in your audience, the first people who come to mind might be friends, teachers, parents, and relatives. That's great, because all of those people are very important members of the audience for your writing. But your audience is much larger than the people you already know. As a writer, your audience is anyone in the world who can read. When I work with students who have trouble thinking of an audience, I tell them to write to famous people and ask them to send a picture and a note. All around the classroom, we display pictures of famous sports stars, business people, authors, and movie actors. All of these people were members of the audience for my students. My students write to Michael Jordan, 'N Sync, the president of the United States, and many other famous people. My students have also written letters to New York City firefighters, police officers, and people serving in the military. Your audience is as big as your imagination.

Now, think of the things that are most important to you. Which audiences would be most likely to share your interest?

I am interested in writing about:

_____

_____

_____

The audience that would most like to read:

_____

_____

_____

_____

_____

_____

_____

Good audiences pay attention. They focus on what the performer, player, or writer is doing and clap for the most important things. When Claudia plays soccer, her audience doesn't clap all the time—just when she makes a goal or a very good pass. Her audience pays careful attention and knows when to clap and when to be quiet. Once I saw a student reading an essay to an adult. Instead of paying attention, the grown-up interrupted and said, "That was great!" The student said, "I haven't even gotten to the good part yet." A good audience member knows it is important to wait until the "good part" before cheering.

Good audiences like being appreciated. At concerts, the audience claps and cheers at the end of the program. Sometimes the people in the audience shout, "Encore!" which is a French word that means "Again!" When this happens, the musicians might play another song, even though the extra song is not on the program. The musicians do this because they want to show the audience that they appreciate the applause just as much as the audience appreciated the great music.

Good audiences for writing need to do all the things that good audiences do for music and sports events. Good audiences for writing also do two important things: They ask questions and make suggestions. The following essay was written by Charlie, a fourth-grade student. Imagine that you are his audience. After reading the essay carefully, give Charlie some applause by writing down what you liked about his essay. Then ask him some questions and make some suggestions.

Sea World

By Charlie

My family and me went to Sea World for vacation. We saw giant killer whales. They were huge!!! My sister didn't want to get spashed so her and Mom and Dad sat in the back, but I sat up front and got soaked. I was so close I could even see their teeth and a gross long tong. Then the trainer let me come up and, you wont' believe this, but I petted the whale—on the nose! I actually felt his skin.

The trainers wore black suiss and were right in the water with the whales, but they didn't get hurt. I also learned that a lot of whales get killed every year and that really makes me mad. They get their tales caught in the net of the fishing boats and then they can't swim and then they die. I was so sad when they talked about this I was crying right in the middle of Sea World, even though everybody else was laughing and having a good time. Then the whales splashed some more and I started laughing again too, but it still makes me mad.

You are the audience. Remember, a good audience member appreciates the hard work of the writer, pays careful attention, asks good questions, and makes specific suggestions.

My Reactions to Charlie's Essay on Sea World

1. Hi, Charlie. Thanks for letting me be the audience for your essay. I really liked the part about . . .

_____

_____

_____

2. Your essay made me think about some questions I'd like to ask you. (Think about who, what, when, where, and especially why.)

_____

_____

_____

_____

_____

3. For your next draft, I'd like to give some suggestions:

_____

_____

_____

_____

Do you think that Charlie's next draft will be better because of your comments? I think so. If you had just said, "Nice job, Charlie—see you later," then he wouldn't know how to improve his writing. Because you took the time to be a good audience, Charlie will take the time to be a better writer. If Charlie were here, he would say, "Thanks!" I hope that when you have an audience for your essays, your audience is as helpful as you were to Charlie.

6 What to Write When You Can't Think of Anything

SOMETIMES teachers tell you what to write about. Other times, you can write about anything you want. That's great—unless you can't think of anything to write about! This chapter will help you think of subjects that are interesting and important for you. Use the lists you make in this chapter any time you feel stuck and unable to think of something to write about. Keep these lists handy. You will probably need them some day!

People I love

_____

_____

_____

_____

_____

Things I love

_____

_____

_____

_____

_____

My favorite foods

_____

_____

_____

_____

_____

_____

Scary animals

_____

_____

_____

_____

_____

_____

Things I know a lot about

_____

_____

_____

_____

_____

Things adults say too often

_____

_____

_____

_____

_____

My favorite books

_____

_____

_____

_____

_____

Now you have lots of different subjects to write about! Next we'll look at ways to turn these subjects into interesting writing ideas.

EXAGGERATION

How can you take a boring subject and make it exciting? One way is to use exaggeration. To use exaggeration, think of an ordinary subject. Think about its basic characteristics and then imagine a wild and silly version of your subject. For example, if you are thinking about a smart dog who likes to do tricks, ask, "What if that dog was smart enough to go to school with me?" Or use yourself as a subject: If you are tall, you might ask, "What if I was as tall as a house?"

Here are some other story starters that take a normal idea and change it into something that is wild and crazy.

How would people treat you if you had eight arms?
What would life be like if we lived in the ocean? On the moon?
What would you remember if you lived to be two hundred years old?
What if you could read people's minds?
What would animals say if they could talk to you?

Now, select a topic from one of the lists you made at the beginning of this chapter. Use the topic to create an ordinary writing idea, and then use exaggeration to turn it into a wild and silly story idea. Here's an example:

Basic story idea: Third-grade kid is a history whiz.

Exaggerated story idea: Third-grade kid is a history whiz because he's three hundred years old and was a friend of George Washington's, conducted experiments with Benjamin Franklin, fought in the Civil War, worked on the transcontinental railroad, helped Thomas Edison invent the lightbulb, suffered through the Great Depression, and now is sitting in a third-grade classroom. The teacher thinks that it's very strange that a kid knows so much about history.

Now, you try it:

Basic story idea:

_____

_____

_____

Exaggerated story idea:

_____

_____

_____

ACTION

Another way to come up with story ideas is to think about action. Ask yourself, "What would happen if this character did things backwards?" You can also think about what would happen if the character suddenly did everything very quickly or very slowly. What would happen if the character could freeze the action in a scene?

PICTURES

Pictures can help you think of new and exciting story ideas. Magazines such as *National Geographic* and *Ranger Rick* are full of great pictures that you can turn into writing topics. In one recent issue of *Ranger Rick,* I found three pictures that gave me ideas for writing assignments:

A squirrel is stretching and yawning, his tongue sticking out, and his paw reaching as far as it can stretch. Did he just get out of bed? Does he want to just go back to sleep and skip squirrel school? Does he daydream about being another animal, like the big creatures with two legs that walk around in his park?

A polar bear, with icicles clinging to the white fur beneath her big black nose and purple tongue. Is she cold? Did she make her fur that way on purpose so that she would look different from the other bears?

A redheaded weaver bird, holding a tiny strand of twine. She is creating a house that is so perfect and neat, it looks like something you would find in a store instead of in the wild. Most birds I have seen just have nests that look like cereal bowls, but this bird has a nest that looks like a three-story tree house. Are some birds more creative than others? Why are their houses different? Why would a bird need a house that is covered on top instead of open on top?

Now you try it. Find a magazine or newspaper picture that is strange or unusual. Use the picture to help you think of ideas, questions, and stories.

Paste your picture here:

Describe the picture in words:

_____

_____

_____

_____

What questions does the picture make you think of?

_____

_____

_____

_____

What stories does the picture make you think of?

_____

_____

_____

_____

USE YOUR IMAGINATION

My oldest son is named Brooks. He is in college now and is a very fine writer. When he was in elementary school, he used to arrange all of his stuffed animals in a circle around him in his room. Then he would invent characters, stories, plots, and actions. He would give each animal a voice, a character, and many ideas. He would throw the animals into the air and, when he was finished playing with them, he would sit down and write a story or a play. Even when he was older, Brooks used his animals to help him think of ideas. You may think you are too old to get ideas from stuffed animals, but you are never too old to have a favorite toy. Use that toy and your imagination to be as creative as you can be.

If your favorite toy could talk, what would it say?

_____

_____

_____

If your toy could move, what would it do?

_____

_____

_____

SPECIAL PLACES FOR YOUR IDEAS

Every writer needs some paper to keep track of ideas, lists, and thoughts. For your next birthday or other special occasion, ask for a journal so that you have a special place to write down your ideas. In our house, we painted one part of a basement wall white and told all the kids in our family that they could write whatever they wanted on that wall (but not on any other walls!). You don't need a wall or a fancy journal to keep track of all your great ideas, but you do need to write them down. It's a great idea to have a pencil and paper with you when you travel, when you are on vacation, when you go to the library, when you go to a museum, or when you are just sitting and thinking. Don't wait for a writing assignment to start collecting your ideas. Your ideas are always important, and they are important right when you are thinking about them.

Let's try it right now. Fill in the blanks in the box below.

The biggest things I have ever seen are:

_____

_____

_____

The smallest things I have ever seen are:

_____

_____

_____

I laughed so hard when . . .

_____

_____

_____

I was kind of mad when . . .

_____

_____

_____

The most interesting animal I have ever seen is . . .

_____

_____

_____

I wish I could be more like . . .

_____

_____

_____

This is stressing me out!

_____

_____

_____

When you can't think of anything to write about, it doesn't feel very good. Some kids feel frustrated and other kids get mad. Most kids get worried if they are supposed to write about something and the words just won't come out. I understand. I'm a writer, just like you. Sometimes I can't think of things to write and, even when I do, the words just come out wrong. When that happens, I remember that I have an audience (that's you), and I think about what they might say. Then I use the ideas in this chapter, like exaggeration, or action, or pictures. Sometimes I even use a toy or a stuffed animal to help me think of something. If you think this sounds silly, go back and read the title of this chapter: "What to Write When You Can't Think of Anything." Then read all the ideas you have written on your work sheets. You can think of a lot of things! Now that you have so many ideas, we need to figure out how to organize them. That is the subject of our next chapter.

Making Sense Out of Nonsense: How to Organize Your Ideas

Your personal rules for good writing probably include a rule about organization. Good writing has a clear beginning, middle, and end. This helps your audience understand your ideas. In this chapter, we will learn to use some tools called graphic organizers. You may have already used some graphic organizers in school. Now you will have a complete tool kit that you can use for any writing assignment.

If organizers are such a good idea, why doesn't everybody use them? Some students are afraid to use graphic organizers because they are in a hurry. They complain, "I don't have time to use an organizer! I've got to get busy and write." This is a mistake. When my students use a graphic organizer, they finish their writing assignments faster and they write better essays and stories. When your writing is well organized, it is easier for the reader to understand your ideas. When you take time to organize your ideas, you will save time on your writing assignments.

Some students don't like to do anything that isn't required. If the teacher doesn't require students to use a graphic organizer, why should they do something extra? That's a fair question. Why should you do anything extra? The reason is that you will be happier with your work when it is well organized. Even if your teacher doesn't require you to use a graphic organizer, do it for yourself. Do you remember Charlie's essay about Sea World? He had some good descriptions of the whales and some important information about the dangers that whales face, but his good ideas were all jumbled together. His essay did not have a clear beginning, middle, and end. When Charlie was writing his essay, it made sense to him. But when he read his essay aloud, it was hard for other students to follow. You could tell that Charlie cared about the whales. He even said that he cried when he learned that some of them died when their tails were caught in a fishnet. But the readers—Charlie's teacher and other students—could not follow Charlie's thinking very well as he jumped from a description of the Sea World performance to details about the problems whales face in the ocean and then back again. If Charlie wants the reader to understand how he feels, he must organize his ideas.

We're going to learn about six types of graphic organizers, and then you will see an example of each one. After each example is a blank graphic organizer that you can copy and use for your own writing projects.

THE DESCRIPTIVE PATTERN ORGANIZER

This is the easiest graphic organizer to use. Place the main idea (your writing topic) in a large circle in the center. Use small circles around the main circle to show details and ideas that support the main idea in the center. (See pages 46 and 47.)

SEQUENCE PATTERN ORGANIZER

Sequence Pattern Organizers are useful when you want to write a story or describe events in the life of a famous person. You can also use this organizer when you want to describe different stages of life for an animal or a plant, or when you want to write about a series of dates in history. The Sequence Pattern Organizer is also helpful if you are working with a group of other students and everybody has different pieces of information that must be placed in order. When you need to organize lots of different pieces of information, it helps to find the very last thing that happened, write it down on the far right-hand side of the Sequence Pattern Organizer, and then work backward to put each piece into place. (See page 48 and 49.)

THE PROCESS/CAUSE PATTERN ORGANIZER

The Process/Cause Pattern Organizer is useful when you need to explain something in an essay. This type of essay is often required in science and social studies classes. Write the final event or end result in the box to the right. (World War II is an example of a final event, and water evaporating is an example of an end result.) What were the events or causes that led to the final event or result? Write the possible causes leading to the final event or result in the circles with the arrows pointing to the box. (See pages 50 and 51.)

THE PROBLEM-SOLUTION PATTERN ORGANIZER

The Problem-Solution Pattern Organizer is a good tool to use when writing a persuasive essay. It will help you think about all the possible solutions to a problem. Good persuasive essays describe several possible solutions to a problem and then tell the reader why one solution is best. When you write a persuasive essay, you must do more than describe how you feel. If you want to be persuasive, you must give the reader good reasons to agree with you. (See pages 52 and 53.)

THE GENERALIZATION PATTERN ORGANIZER

The Generalization Pattern Organizer helps you test your ideas to see if they are true even when you change some of the details. For example, a writer might state that the sun causes evaporation. Does that mean that if we had a bowl of water inside the house where there was no sunlight that the water would not evaporate? In the Generalization Pattern Organizer, you write the statement that you think is true at the top, and then write statements in the boxes underneath that contain facts that may or may not agree with your general statement. If the facts do not support the statement, then the general statement is false and must be revised until it is true. (See pages 54 and 55.)

THE CONCEPT PATTERN ORGANIZER

The Concept Pattern Organizer is a good way to help you organize ideas for a longer essay, writing assignment, or other project. You can use the Concept Pattern Organizer if you have many different ideas, facts, and examples to put in your outline. (See pages 56 and 57.)

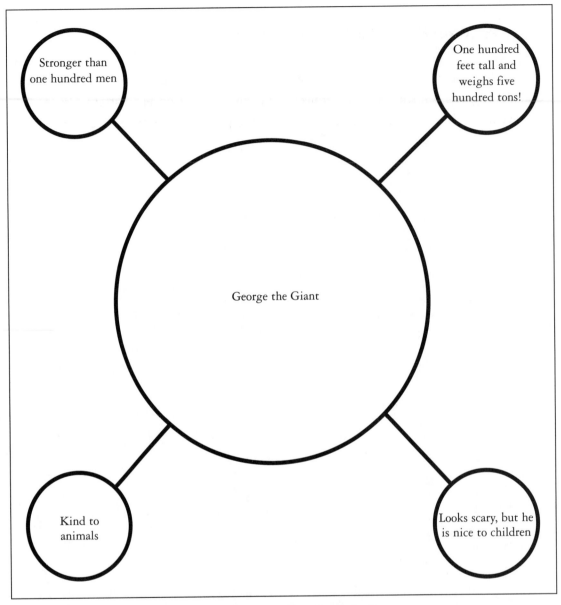

Figure 7.1a. My Story About George the Giant

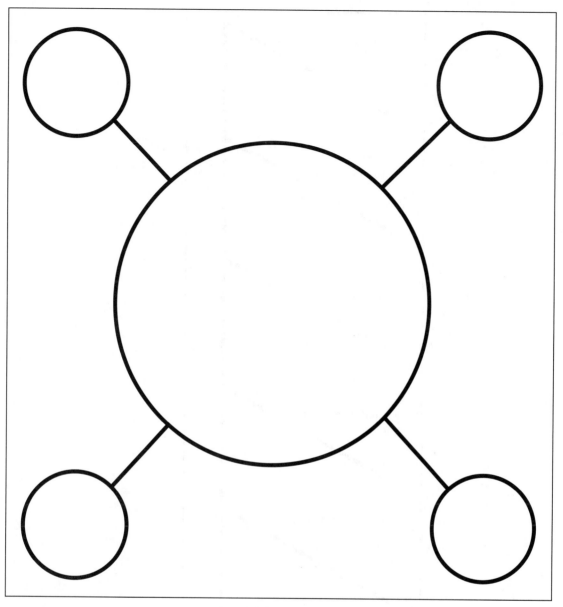

Figure 7.1b. The Descriptive Pattern

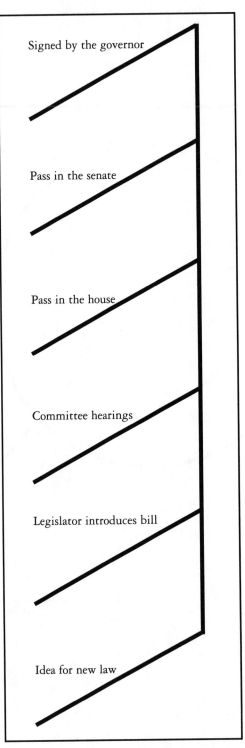

Signed by the governor

Pass in the senate

Pass in the house

Committee hearings

Legislator introduces bill

Idea for new law

Figure 7.2a. How an Idea Becomes a Law

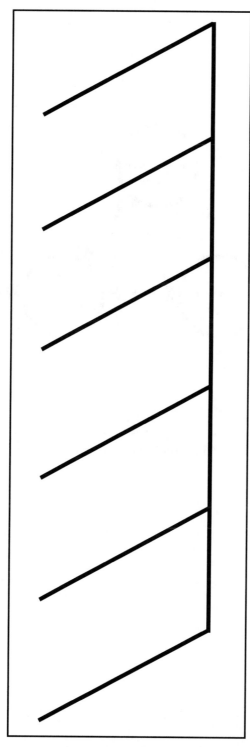

Figure 7.2b. The Sequence Pattern

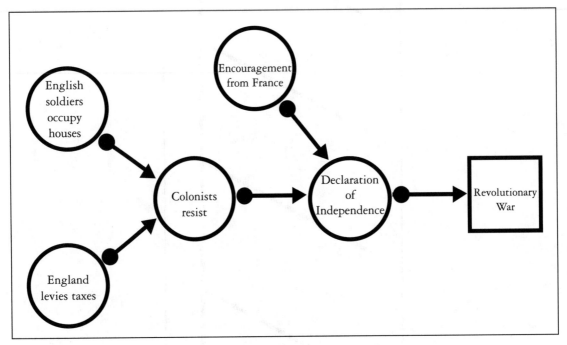

Figure 7.3a. What Caused the American Revolution?

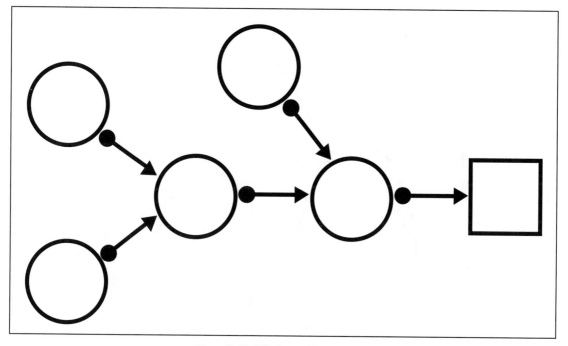

Figure 7.3b. The Process/Cause Pattern

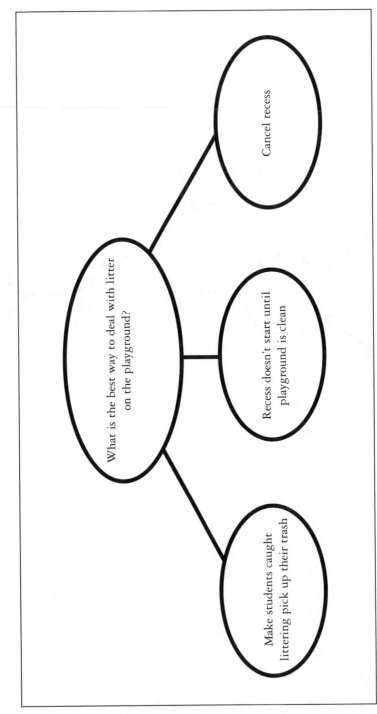

Figure 7.4a. Litter on the Playground

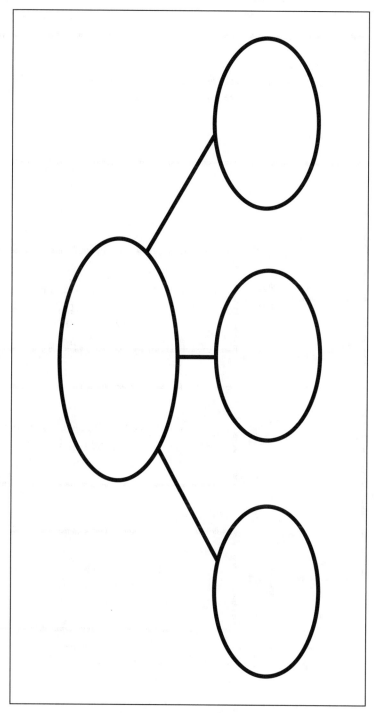

Figure 7.4b. The Problem-Solution Pattern

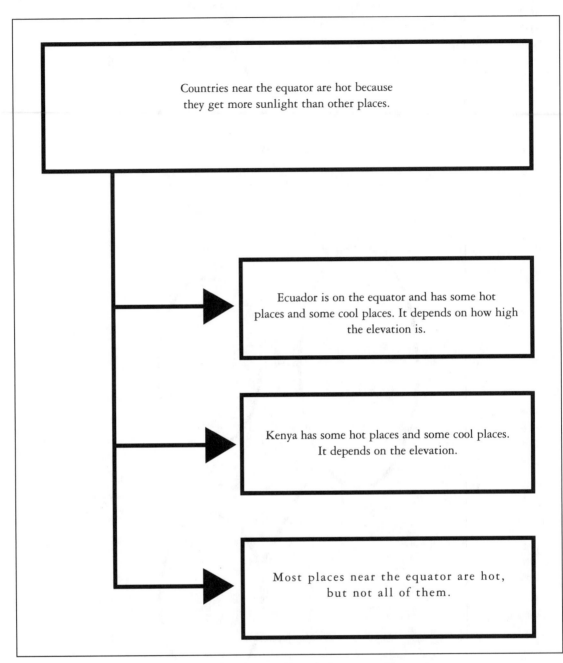

Countries near the equator are hot because
they get more sunlight than other places.

Ecuador is on the equator and has some hot
places and some cool places. It depends on how high
the elevation is.

Kenya has some hot places and some cool places.
It depends on the elevation.

Most places near the equator are hot,
but not all of them.

Figure 7.5a. Countries Near the Equator are Hot

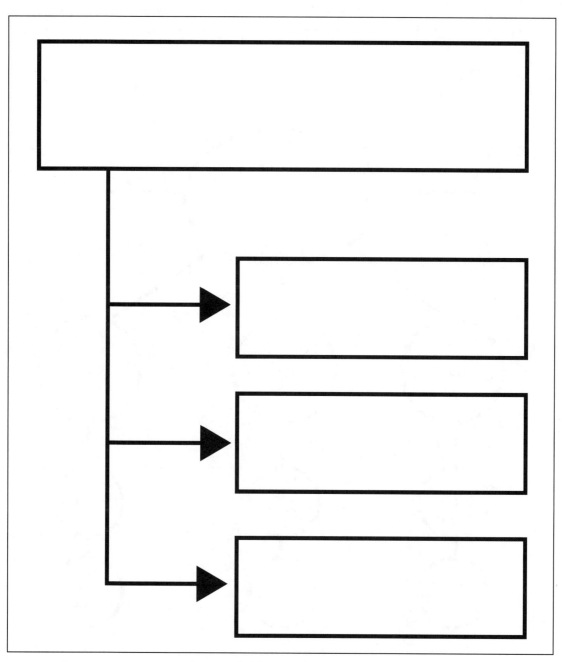

Figure 7.5b. The Generalization Pattern

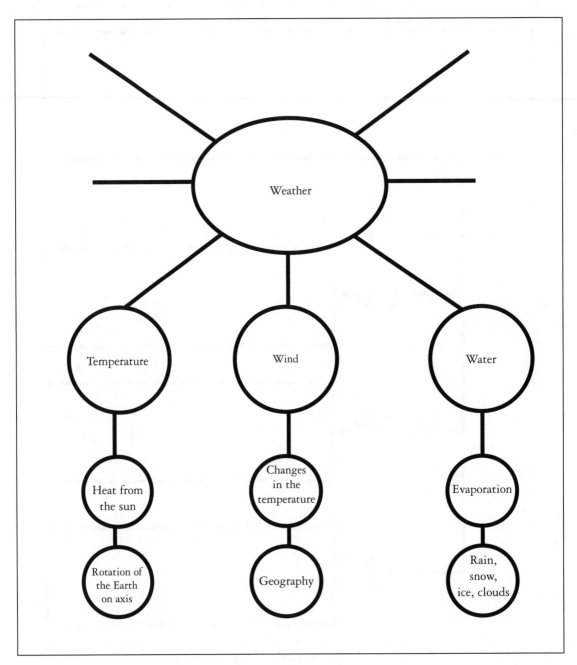

Figure 7.6a. All About the Weather

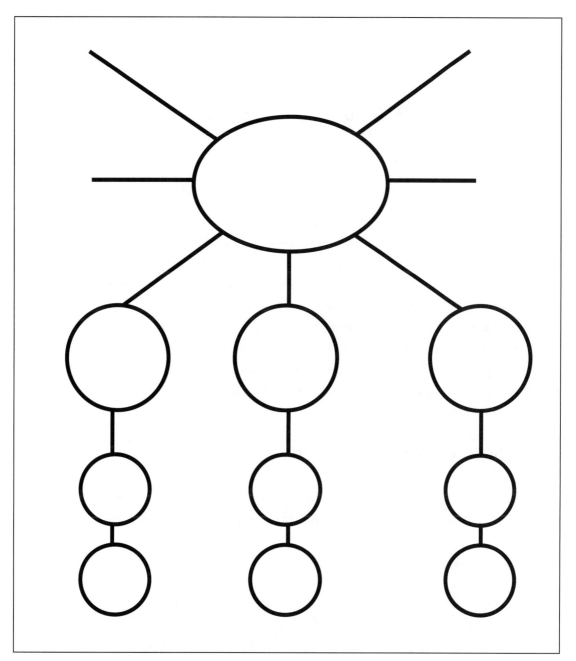

Figure 7.6b. The Concept Pattern

8 Why Can't I Just Use the Computer?

COMPUTERS are great. With a computer, you can play games, draw pictures, make charts, and write letters and essays. You probably already know how to use a computer, and you may even use one every day at home or in school. If you use a computer often, you probably know that you can write faster on a computer than you can with a pencil. You may find it easier to use the spell checker on your computer than a dictionary. In this chapter, we will talk about the best way to use a computer to write stories, essays, and letters. We will also talk about why it is still important for you to be able to write stories, essays, and letters without a computer.

GUIDELINES FOR USING THE COMPUTER

If you want to use the computer for your writing assignments, that's fine. But these are some rules you should follow in order to be the best writer you can be.

Turn Off the Automatic Spell Checker

This may seem strange. "Why shouldn't I use a tool that helps me correct my spelling?" you may ask. The reason I want you to turn the spell checker off is that their are many misspellings your spell checker won't catch. Did you notice the mistake in the last sentence? I wrote *their* instead of *there,* and the computer spell checker would say that both words are spelled correctly. But only one of the words—*there*—is correct. The most important reason to turn the spell checker off is that every student must learn the skills of proofreading, editing, and correcting errors. The only way to learn these skills is to practice them. As you become an expert editor and proofreader, it may be helpful to use the spell checker in the future. But for now, please turn it off.

Use Large Font Sizes, Such as 14- to 16-Point Type

The "font" is the style of type that you use. For example, here are three words in different font types. Which one is the easiest for you to read?

Penguin

Penguin

Penguin

It's fun to play with different font styles, but it's always important to pick a font style that is easy to read. It's also important to use whatever font style your teacher asks you to use for class work.

The font size tells you how large the print is. For example, here are letters in 10-point, 14-point, and 18-point type. Which one is easier to read?

"I love to write!"

"I love to write!"

"I love to write!"

It is a good idea to use 14-point type through the third grade. Fourteen-point type is also a good size for letters. It is especially helpful if you are writing to a grandparent or other person who finds larger print easier to read. Starting in fourth grade, your teachers may prefer that you use 12-point type. Most teachers will tell you exactly which font size they want you to use.

Use Triple Spacing Through the Third Grade and Double Spacing After the Third Grade

The "spacing" is a measure of the amount of blank space between each line of text. Single spacing means that there are no blank lines between the lines of text, like this:

The ducks waddled down the street, with the baby ducks following the mother. Like soldiers marching in line, the ducklings followed their leader in single file.

Double spacing means that there is one blank line between each line of text, like this:

The birds were working quickly to build their nest. Using straw, grass,

and even pieces of string, they put the nest together bit by bit until, in less

than an hour, they had created their new home.

Triple spacing means that there are two blank lines between each line of text, so that text appears on every third line. The reason to use triple spacing through the third grade is that it leaves more room for you, your parents, and your teacher to make marks, ask questions, and make revisions on your paper. It is difficult for your teacher to add marks or write notes on your paper when it is single-spaced. If you use triple spacing (or, after third grade, double spacing), there will be room for you, other students, your teacher, or your parents to make marks without covering up your writing.

Handwriting Is Still Important

Students like to use computers because computers make their work look neat. The computer printer makes letters that are much neater than any student's handwriting. Computers are convenient and helpful, but you still need to be able to write legibly by hand. Some tests require handwritten answers, and letters to friends and family always mean more when they are handwritten.

I advise a newspaper club for third-, fourth-, and fifth-grade students. When they are preparing a story, the students make handwritten notes in their "reporter's notebooks," which they carry to the scene of every story they cover. The first draft of every story is written by hand, and then club members work together to edit and revise the stories, still using pencil and paper. It's easier to cross out words and play with ideas when you can see all of your revisions on the page. If you were using a computer, you wouldn't be able to see your original work along with your revisions.

The students in the newspaper club are expert computer users. They use word processing programs for their stories and create graphs, tables, charts, and pictures to illustrate their stories. However, their stories always begin with handwritten notes in their reporter's notebooks.

9 You're the Teacher: How to Evaluate Your Own Writing

Y‍OU have probably met some teachers who are really good at helping kids learn. Great teachers can be found at school, coaching sports after school, giving music lessons, and leading scout troops. You have probably been a teacher, too. Have you ever helped a friend learn a new game or shown a classmate how to use a computer program? In a minute, I'm going to ask you to think about your best experience as a student. I will also ask you about your best experience as a teacher. I will ask you to remember how a teacher helped you improve, and I will ask you how you helped a student improve.

Before I ask you to write about your experiences as a student and as a teacher, I will share my own experiences with you. Even though I have been a teacher for many years, I am also still a student, just like you. I love it when my teachers tell me that I'm doing a good job, and I feel uncomfortable when they say I didn't do as well as I could have. The teachers who help me the most are the ones who tell me exactly how to get better and exactly what they like about my work. They don't just say, "Nice job!" and then go on to the next student. They tell me how I can do better the next time.

Now, take a minute to think about your best experience as a student. Perhaps it was in a class in school or perhaps it was when you played on a sports team or took a music lesson. Whenever it was, you felt great because you learned something and you almost surprised yourself at how good you were. Think about that experience and complete these sentences:

My Best Experience as a Student

My teacher was named: _____

I felt great because I:

_____

_____

My teacher told me (try to remember the exact words):

_____

_____

I think that I can do even better next time because:

_____

_____

Now, think about your best experience when you were the teacher helping another student (or even an adult) to learn something new.

My Best Experience as a Teacher

My student was named: _____

My student felt great because:

_____

_____

I told my student (try to remember the exact words):

_____

_____

I think that my student can do even better next time because:

_____

_____

Your experiences as a student and a teacher will help you understand how to become a better writer. Of course, it is helpful when someone else looks at your writing and gives you ideas for improving it. But most of the time you will be your own reviewer. You need to learn how to evaluate your own writing even when a teacher is not there to help you.

GUIDELINES FOR EVALUATING WRITING

When you evaluate your own writing or the writing of another student, here are some important guidelines to remember:

Be Specific

Identify exactly what you liked and what you think should be changed. If you were checking your own writing, you might say, "I really liked the description of the main character, and I'm going to keep that. I also liked the organization. There was a clear beginning, middle, and end." Then you can add, "But my writing seems to be kind of dull. Maybe that is because the words I am using do not have a lot of action. I'm going to circle some words that I can replace with more exciting words that will grab the reader's interest."

Be Fair to Yourself and to Anyone Else You Evaluate

What does it mean to be fair? When you play a game with your friends, you all agree on the rules of the game at the beginning, and it would be unfair if someone tried to change the rules in the middle of the game. The same is true with writing. You have to know the rules of good writing and apply them every time you evaluate your writing or another student's writing. You can't say, "Well, spelling really isn't important now," or "I tried pretty hard, so I guess I don't have to be organized." The rules are the rules, and if you are going to be fair, you have to apply the rules every time.

You Have to be Accurate

If you were checking your answers on a math test and you saw that you had written "5 + 5 = 11," what would you do? I don't think you would say, "Well, I know it's wrong, but I don't want to change my answer." You would erase the "11" and change your answer to "10" because you know that one is wrong and the other is right. That's being accurate. There's just one problem. Everybody knows that "5 + 5 = 10," but not everybody knows what "good writing" is supposed to be. What's the best way to know, especially if different people have different opinions? That's what the rest of this chapter is all about.

SCORING GUIDES: THE BEST WAY TO EVALUATE YOUR WRITING

The best way to improve your writing is with a scoring guide. A scoring guide describes what great writing is. It also describes writing that is okay, writing that is pretty good but not quite good enough, and writing that does not meet the standards of good writing.

Your teacher probably uses a scoring guide to grade papers and tests. Your teacher may call it a "rubric" or some other name. Whatever it is called, your teacher has a system for evaluating writing. This is important: If your teacher uses a scoring guide, then you must use that scoring guide whenever you evaluate your writing. This is not just for a big test or an important writing assignment. Using your teacher's scoring guide will help you improve your writing every single time you write. If your teacher does not use a scoring guide, you can still use scoring guides created by other people or one that you create yourself. If you want to know how your state evaluates writing, look for this information on your state department of education's Web site.

You don't have to use an official scoring guide. You can make your own. Here is one that was created by some student writers in the third, fourth, and fifth grades.

Source: The Stanley School Newspaper Club

	BASIC ("I'm working on it.")	PROGRESSING ("I'm almost there.")	PROFICIENT ("I did it!")	EXEMPLARY ("Knocked my socks off!")
Organization	The reader can't understand what the writer intends to say.	The topic sentence tells the reader what to expect, but there is not a clear beginning, middle, and end.	There is a clear beginning, middle, and end.	There is a clear beginning, middle, and end, with transitions between each section.
Conventions	The reader can't understand what the writer intends to say.	The spelling and punctuation mistakes sometimes prevent the reader from understanding what the writer intends.	There are a few mistakes, but they do not prevent the reader from understanding what the writer intends.	There are no errors in grammar, spelling, or punctuation.

Figure 9.1 Sample Scoring Guide

You can use this scoring guide to evaluate your own writing or when you evaluate another student's work. It will help you give help and feedback that is specific, fair, and accurate. For example, with the scoring guide, you might say to a friend (or to yourself):

"I noticed that your story had a clear beginning, middle, and end. That's great. It means that your writing was very organized. In the first sentence, I understood what the paragraph was about. In the middle you gave me some important details. And at the end, you let me know why all of those details were important. I also noticed that some of the sentences didn't start with a capital letter and that you probably guessed at some of the spelling. That's okay, but for your next draft, can you check the words that I underlined in the dictionary to make sure that your spelling is accurate? You already know about capitals at the beginning of a sentence, so I expect you to fix those mistakes on your own. It's a great story, and I can't wait to see the next draft."

Now you try it. Read the paragraph in the box below and provide feedback to the writer that is specific, fair, and accurate.

Who Makes the Laws

I always wondered who makes the laws. Some people complain about them and other people like them. So how do ideas become laws that we all have to obey?

In our state, the legislature makes the laws. The people elect the members of the legislature and they meet in the state capital every winter. If one of the senators or representatives has an idea, then they write it down and a committee looks at it. I watched the education committee look at a bill and it was hundreds of pages long. Some people said the bill was a good idea and some people said it was a terrible idea. Then the committee voted on the bill and they liked it so then the bill went to the whole legislature and then they voted on it and they liked it and then it became a law, but only after the governor signed it. Not everybody liked it. One senator, Mr. Quinlan, yelled about it and called the law a disgrace and his face was red when he talked. Then another man told him to calm down and said it was good. Then woman who was also a senator said that it was good and another man said he didn't understand it but he was sure it was ok. I was hoping to hear about a law about animals or old people or the Rain Forest or something but all they talked about was the education law, so I just listened and that's how a law is made. When you walk into the state capital building, there is a HUGE picture of John Brown and his eyes bulge out and he looks so mad! Every day the senators have to walk right past that picture. But the rest of the capital is very pretty.

I liked the part where you:

_____

_____

_____

I noticed that you:

_____

_____

_____

I'd like to ask you:

_____

_____

_____

I think that your writing would be even better if you would:

_____

_____

_____

Now, try this with a piece of your own writing. Try to use a school assignment, but you can also use a letter or any writing that you have done just for yourself. Take a minute to read what you have written, and then give yourself some feedback that is specific, accurate, and fair:

I liked the part where I:

_____

_____

_____

I noticed that I:

_____

_____

_____

I'd like to ask myself:

_____

_____

I think that my writing would be even better if I would:

_____

_____

_____

Use this system to evaluate all of your writing, including homework assignments, letters, journal entries, and stories you write for fun. It will help you become a better writer very quickly. It is easier to become a better writer when you know the rules of good writing and are careful to follow them.

10 Dear Mr. President: Writing Letters to Get a Response

WHEN we talk, we want someone to listen to us. In school and at home, kids say things all the time, but sometimes it seems like no one is listening. It's frustrating. After a while, some kids just stop talking unless they are sure somebody is listening. Here is the best thing about writing: Even if nobody is around, somebody is listening to you. When you write letters, you know that somebody is listening to you because they write back. Writing letters is one of the most exciting, interesting, and powerful things that anybody can do.

I'm not going to tell you who to write to—choose anybody you want. You can write to your parents. If you tucked letters under their pillows before they went to bed, it would be the best surprise they have had in a long time. You can write to a relative. They love getting mail just as much as you do. You can write to the president or your governor, mayor, legislator, school board member, or other public official. They care about what you think and will probably write back to you. You can write to your teacher or to someone who was your teacher last year or even before that. Teachers love to get letters from students. You can write to people you admire. Since September 11, 2001, many students have written letters to police officers, firefighters, nurses, doctors, ambulance workers, and people in the military. You can write to your favorite athlete, author, artist, musician, movie star, or poet. You can write to companies that make products you use. You can even write to me. I get lots of letters from students, parents, and teachers, and I reply to every one of them. The addresses for people you might want to write to are at the end of this chapter.

It's fun to get mail. But if you want to receive mail, you need to send it. Take a minute and make a list of five people that you would like to receive a letter from.

I would like to get a letter from:

_____

_____

_____

_____

_____

Now make another list of people whom you want to thank. You might want to thank a relative who sent you a gift or someone who helps you all the time, such as a librarian, sports coach, or school crossing guard. You might also want to thank someone who helps your community, such as a hospital worker, zookeeper, or lifeguard.

I would like to thank:

_____

_____

_____

_____

_____

Writing letters is just like playing a musical instrument or playing a sport. You will get better and better with practice. With practice, you will learn to include important details in your letters. Since you know you will have an audience for your letters (just as you have an audience for musical performances or at sporting events), you will put extra thought and effort into your letters. Writing letters is not just an interesting thing to do. Writing letters will make you a better writer.

THE RULES OF GOOD LETTER WRITING

If you want your reader to pay attention to your letter, you need to follow the rules of good letter writing. Good letters include:

- The sender's street address, city, state, and zip code in the top right-hand corner. (If you don't include your address, you won't get a letter back.)

- The date (in the top right corner, one line below the sender's address).

- The addressee's full name and address (on the left-hand side of the page, one line below the date). Note: You can leave this out if you are writing to a friend or relative.

- A greeting ("Dear Aunt Sally," or "Dear Mr. Jordan:") followed by a comma (for friends and relatives) or a colon (for letters to companies and strangers).

- A clear statement about the purpose of the letter: "Thank you for the book you sent for my birthday," or "I really like your sneakers and would like to know more about how they are made."

- A complimentary close ("Sincerely," or "Love,").

- A neat signature.

- Legible handwriting (word processing is okay for letters to companies), correct spelling, grammar, and punctuation.

ADDRESSES

Ask your parents or teacher to help you find addresses for the letters that you write. On pages 73–75 are some addresses that will help you start writing letters.

Authors

J. K. Rowling (the *Harry Potter* series), Ann
M. Martin (the *Baby-sitter's Club* series), K. A.
Applegate (*Animorphs, Everworld*), R. L. Stine
(*Goosebumps*):

Author's Name
c/o Scholastic, Inc.
557 Broadway
New York, NY 10012

• • •

Judy Blume (*Tales of a Fourth Grade Nothing*),
Christopher Awdry (the more recent *Thomas
the Tank Engine* series), Marc Brown (the
Arthur series), Stan and Jan Berenstain
(*Berenstain Bears* series):

Author's Name
c/o Random House Children's Publishing
1540 Broadway
New York, NY 10036

• • •

Maurice Sendak (*Where the Wild Things Are*),
Beverly Cleary (*Ramona*):

Author's Name
c/o HarperCollins Children's Books
1350 Avenue of the Americas
New York, NY 10019

• • •

Ian Falconer (the *Olivia* series), Judith Viorst
(*Alexander and the Terrible, Horrible, No Good,
Very Bad Day*):

Author's Name
c/o Simon & Schuster Children's Books
1230 Avenue of the Americas
New York, NY 10020

• • •

Madeleine L'Engle (*A Wrinkle in Time*):

Farrar, Straus, and Giroux
19 Union Square West
New York, NY 10003

Animal Helpers

If you care about animals, you can write to
these magazines and tell them how you feel.

Ranger Rick Magazine
National Wildlife Federation
11100 Wildlife Center Drive
Reston, VA 20190-5362

World Wildlife Fund
1250 24th Street NW
Washington, D.C. 20037

National Geographic World
National Geographic
P.O. Box 98199
Washington, D.C. 20090-8199

Newspapers and Magazines

You can write a letter to the editor of your local newspaper or to some of these excellent magazines.

Stone Soup
Children's Art Foundation
P.O. Box 83
Santa Cruz, CA 95063

Cricket
Cobblestone Publications
30 Grove Street, Suite C
Peterborough, NH 03458

Highlights for Children
P.O. Box 18275
Columbus, OH 43218

*U*S* Kids*
Benjamin Franklin Literary and Medical Society
1100 Waterway Boulevard
Indianapolis, IN 46206

Companies Whose Products You Use

Companies always want to know what their customers think of their products. Think of a company whose products you like—or don't like—and write to tell them why.

Food Companies

McDonald's

McDonald's
Customer Relations
Kroc Drive
Oak Brook, IL 60523

Pizza Hut

Pizza Hut
Customer Relations
14841 Dallas Parkway
Dallas, TX 75254

Taco Bell

Taco Bell
Consumer Affairs
17901 Von Karmen
Irvine, CA 92614

Sneaker Companies

Nike

Nike World Headquarters
Consumer Affairs
One Bowerman Drive
Beaverton, OR 97005-6453

Reebok

Reebok International Ltd.
Customer Relations
P.O. Box 1060
Ronks, PA 17573

Television Networks

Check each station's Web site for information about contacting individual shows.

ABC Television Network

ABC, Inc.
Viewer Relations
500 S. Buena Vista Street
Burbank, CA 91521-4551
Web site: *abc.abcnews.go.com*

CBS Television Network

CBS Television Network
Viewer Relations
51 West 52nd Street
New York, NY 10019
Web site: *www.cbs.com*

FOX Television

FOX Broadcasting
Viewer Relations
P.O. Box 900
Beverly Hills, CA 90213
Web site: *www.fox.com*

NBC Television

NBC Television
Viewer Relations
30 Rockefeller Plaza
New York, NY 10112
Web site: *www.nbc.com*

Tell Me About It: Writing to Describe People, Places, Events, and Things

I F I asked you what you did in school today, what would you say? If you are like most kids, including mine, you would probably answer, "Nothing." But you and I know that a lot of things happened, and when you think about them, those things are important and interesting. In this chapter, you will write about subjects that are important to you. For each writing project, you will choose a topic, think about important details for your description, and then write your essay.

DESCRIBING PEOPLE

Your first essay will be a description of a person. You can choose anyone you wish—a sister or brother, parent, grandparent, teacher, neighbor, or anyone else. Before you start writing your essay, list all the details that will make your description interesting for you and the reader.

This essay is about:

_____

This person is important to me because:

_____

_____

Some special things about this person are:

_____

_____

_____

Here is a word picture of this person:

_____

_____

_____

This person does interesting things such as:

_____

_____

_____

This person says interesting things such as:

_____

_____

_____

I enjoy spending time with this person because:

_____

_____

_____

Other things that are important about this person are:

_____

_____

_____

Great job! Because you took the time to think about your special person, you can now write a description that will be interesting and complete.

A Special Person

_____

_____

_____

_____

_____

_____

_____

_____

_____

DESCRIBING EVENTS

Think of an event that is important to you. It might be something that happened in school, at home, or while you were playing. Your important event could also be something that you learned about—perhaps an event in the news, sports, or your community. First, list the details of the event and then write your essay describing it.

Title: _____

What happened?

_____

_____

_____

Where did it happen?

_____

When did it happen?

_____

How did it happen?

_____

_____

_____

Why did it happen?

_____

_____

_____

What happened before this event that would help the reader understand it?

_____

_____

_____

What happened after this event that would help the reader understand why it is important?

_____

_____

_____

Why is this event important to you?

_____

_____

Now that you have organized your ideas, write an essay describing this event:

An Important Event

_____

_____

_____

_____

_____

_____

_____

_____

Congratulations! You have written two descriptive essays. Ask a friend, parent, or teacher to read your work and then ask questions and make suggestions. When I read a descriptive essay, I almost always want to know more. I ask the writer to tell me more details. I also want to know how the writer feels about the event or person in the essay. Listen to your readers and then think about how you can make your next essay even better.

12 Help Me Understand: Writing to Explain

MOST of your writing assignments in elementary school ask you to write fiction—made-up stories that you create—or descriptive stories about your personal experiences. These types of writing are important, but you need practice with other types of writing as well. One of the most important types of writing is called "analytical" writing. Some schools call this "informational" writing or "expository" writing. Whatever you call it, the purpose is the same: to help the reader understand something.

There are three types of analytical writing: parts of a whole, cause and effect, and similarities and differences. You can practice each type of analytical writing in the next few pages.

PARTS OF A WHOLE

Think about dirt. At first, dirt looks like a lump of brown stuff that you wipe off your shoes before you go inside the house. But take a closer look. Put a few pinches of dirt on a white piece of paper. Spread it out carefully and look at it closely. What do you see? If you have a magnifying glass or, better yet, a microscope, look at the dirt again, very slowly and carefully. Is it still just a blob of brown stuff, or do you see different colors? Is it all the same shape, or do you see different pieces with different shapes? Is it all just dirt or do you see little pieces of rock, sand, grass, or other materials? When scientists analyze something, they try to understand the different parts of what they are analyzing. Even something that looks simple—like a glass of water—is really made up of two different types of atoms, hydrogen and oxygen. When you write to explain something, you can use the "parts of a whole" process to help the reader understand how things are made. Let's try it. Choose a topic from the following list:

Box of cereal
Toy car
Piano
Calculator
Meat loaf
Television
Song
Swing set

In the box below, write down the parts that make up the thing you have selected. Write a few words that describe each part. Sometimes you will discover that what you thought was one part is actually several parts. For example, the cord on the television isn't just one piece, but it has two wires, the plastic that covers the wires, the plug, and three metal pieces that go from the plug into the wall. If you discover that a part is made up of other parts, then create smaller boxes on the right to list each part. Those are the "parts of parts." The more careful you are in your analysis, the more different parts you will discover.

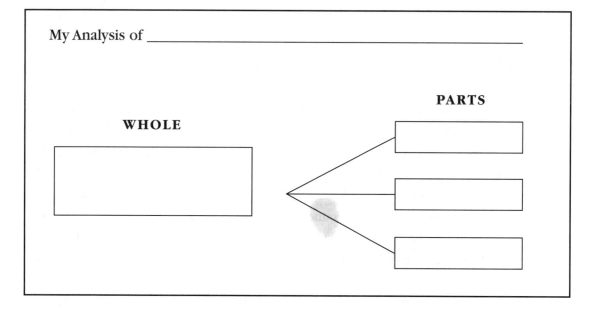

My Analysis of _____

PARTS

WHOLE

Great job! Now that you have listed the parts, and the parts of each part, write an essay analyzing what you have. Your reader will be amazed at how many details you included.

_____

_____

_____

_____

_____

_____

_____

_____

CAUSE AND EFFECT

If you have a little brother or sister, you have probably heard him or her ask "why" about a hundred times. Sometimes it seems that is the only word little kids know. Each time you give them an answer, they again ask, "Why?" It's a pretty smart question, even from a three-year-old kid. Older kids like you also ask "why" questions. Why is the sky blue? Why do birds sing? Why do some cars appear to have smoke coming out of their tailpipes? Why does the moon move around the sky? Why do animals have different kinds of teeth? You probably discuss the answers to lots of "why" questions in social studies class. Why did the American colonies declare independence? Why did the Civil War start? Why did people once own slaves?

Think about the last time you asked a "why" question. Did you get a detailed answer, or did someone say, "That's just the way it is"? If you didn't get a detailed answer, then you didn't get to learn very much and you didn't get a very good answer to your question. Now you are the one answering the "why" question, and you can do a much more complete job. Think of five questions that begin with "why." The questions can be about any subjects that interest you. They can be about nature, history, people, weather, or anything else that you find interesting.

1. Why

_____

2. Why

_____

3. Why

_____

4. Why

_____

5. Why

_____

Now, select one of your questions and use a copy of the Process/Cause Pattern Organizer on page 51 to help you plan your writing.

Take a close look at your graphic organizer. Have you answered the "why" question? Do you have several different causes? Do you need to add some more details? When you have reviewed your graphic organizer and made it as complete as possible, you are ready to write your analytical essay.

_____

_____

_____

_____

_____

_____

_____

_____

_____

COMPARE AND CONTRAST

Many tests and homework assignments include essay questions. Essay questions give you a chance to "show what you know" by explaining things in writing. In middle school, many essay questions begin with the instruction "compare and contrast." This means that you need to explain how two things are similar (compare) and how they are different (contrast). You may not be in middle school yet, but it's not too early to learn how to write a "compare and contrast" essay. If you practice now, you will have a much easier time in middle school.

You may already have written a "compare and contrast" essay, and you certainly have thought about how things are similar and how they are different. When you see the words *compare and contrast,* remember that you need to explain how the two things are similar and how they are different. For example, you might be asked to, "Compare and contrast a movie and the book on which the movie was based." You could decide to write about the book *Harry Potter and the Sorcerer's Stone* and the movie based on it. First, you need to list all the ways that they are similar, then all the ways that they are different. You may want to make a judgment about which you liked better, the movie or the book.

When we compare and contrast, we understand things better. You can compare and contrast different characters in stories, novels, fables, and movies. (Compare and contrast the heroine of the *Matilda* books with the heroine of *The Little House on the Prairie*.) You can compare and contrast different events in history (World War I and the Vietnam War). You can compare and contrast different places (your hometown and a place you visited on vacation). You can even compare and contrast different people (your mother and your grandmother). This chapter includes a chart that will help you organize your ideas for a "compare and contrast" essay. Copy this chart and use it whenever you need to compare and contrast two things. Use it now to organize your ideas for a compare and contrast essay about any topics you like. If you can't think of a topic, choose one from the list at the end of this chapter. The key is that you must be able to list some things that are similar and some things that are different.

Compare this:_____	To this: _____
How is it similar?	**How is it similar?**
How is it different?	**How is it different?**

Figure 12.1 Compare and Contrast ("T-Chart")

Great job! Now you are ready to write your essay. This will probably be the longest essay you have written so far. You will have at least three paragraphs: an introduction, a paragraph about similarities, and a paragraph about differences. You may also want to add a final paragraph that gives a conclusion or tells which of the two things you prefer.

_____

_____

_____

_____

_____

_____

_____

_____

_____

_____

_____

_____

_____

_____

_____

_____

_____

_____

Writing analytical essays will get easier if you practice. And the more you practice writing and revising your essays, the better your essays will be. In the box titled "Analytical Essay Prompts," you will find some other ideas for analytical writing.

ANALYTICAL ESSAY PROMPTS

Parts of a Whole

1. Car engines
2. My favorite toy
3. My family
4. Flowers
5. Our solar system
6. My favorite food
7. A quilt
8. Skyscrapers
9. My favorite song
10. A sports team

Cause and Effect

1. Sunrises
2. Seasons
3. The common cold
4. Why I get mad/happy/sad
5. Why the Civil War started
6. Why some Native Americans live on reservations
7. Why Social Security exists
8. Leap year
9. What causes lightbulbs to shine
10. What makes me do my very best work

Compare/Contrast

1. Harry Potter's two best friends (Hermione and Ron)
2. Batman and Superman
3. My two favorite movies
4. My two favorite books
5. My two favorite sports teams
6. Modern armies and Sauran's forces (from Tolkien's *The Lord of the Rings*)
7. Barbie and G.I. Joe
8. My life and my parents' lives when they were my age
9. My best friend and me
10. My house and my grandparents' house

13 I'm Mad! Writing to Influence Other People

How do you feel about school uniforms? What about littering? How about cruelty to animals? Some things really make you mad. As a writer, you can do something about them. You can write persuasive essays that change the opinions and actions of other people. If you want to influence people, you must write with feeling and power. You already have the feelings—perhaps you are mad, sad, or worried. Now you need to add power to your feelings so that you can write a great persuasive essay. Your essay needs evidence—facts and examples—as well as feelings if you want to persuade your reader to change an opinion or take action.

The keys to a good persuasive essay are contained in the code word PEAS. PEAS stands for Problem, Evidence, Arguments, and Solution. When you write a persuasive essay, create a separate paragraph for each of these letters. In the first paragraph, tell the reader exactly what the problem is. You can also give the reader a hint about the evidence, arguments, and solutions that you are going to present in the other paragraphs. The second paragraph should contain the most powerful part of your essay—the evidence. Do not use the words "I feel" in this paragraph. Stick to the facts and provide some examples. Facts and examples tell the reader why the problem is serious and why a solution is necessary. In the third paragraph, provide your arguments. Your arguments should tell the reader why a solution is necessary or why the reader should take action. The fourth paragraph should explain your solution. Now that you've explained the problem, what do you want the reader to do?

If you were writing a persuasive essay about the problem of children not eating properly, your first paragraph would describe how serious the problem is. Your second paragraph would present some important facts: Forty-two percent of school children do not receive all the vitamins they need, more than half of all children do not eat a good breakfast, and poor eating habits cause illness and learning problems in children. The arguments in your third paragraph would explain to the reader why the facts prove that childhood nutrition is an important issue and why the reader should be concerned about it. In the fourth paragraph, you would describe a solution, such as classes for parents and students about good eating habits.

Choose a problem that is important to you and write a persuasive essay about it. First, remember PEAS: List your problem, evidence, arguments, and solution. Then write your persuasive essay. Take some time for the "E" paragraph. Finding evidence is sometimes hard and takes some time. This would be a good project to do in the library, where the librarian can help you. You can also find evidence in newspaper or magazine articles, on the Internet, or using resources at school. Remember: You cannot write a good persuasive essay without good evidence, facts, and examples to support your ideas.

Planning a Persuasive Essay: PEAS

P—Problem

_____

_____

E—Evidence (facts, examples, statistics)

_____

_____

_____

_____

_____

A—Arguments (What do the facts tell us and what conclusions can we draw?)

_____

_____

_____

S—Solution (What action do you want the reader to do?)

_____

_____

_____

Persuasive Essay

_____

_____

_____

_____

_____

_____

_____

_____

_____

14 Research Papers Without Pain

RESEARCH papers used to be just for high school and college students. Today, many fourth- and fifth-grade students are required to write research papers that are four or five pages long. The papers use research from books, magazines, the Internet, and other sources. Students must include a list of references they used when writing the paper. If you are lucky enough to have a teacher who requires a research paper, don't be angry. Writing a research paper now will help you get ready for middle school. When you have to write research papers in the future, you will know what to expect. And when many of your classmates are nervous and anxious, you will be cool and calm.

WHY DOES MY PAPER NEED FOOTNOTES AND REFERENCE LISTS?

If someone told you an amazing fact, what would you say? Probably, "How do you know that's true?" If the person could show you the fact in a reliable book or a magazine, you'd believe it. Books and magazines contain valuable information that we could not get on our own. We couldn't create a detailed map of the moon or count the population of Tanzania ourselves. When you use facts and information from books for your research paper, you need to show your reader that they come from an accurate, up-to-date source.

There is another important reason to tell the reader where you found your information. When you credit your sources, you are not just a good writer—you are an honest writer. You wouldn't take a toy or a book that belonged to someone else. That would be stealing. It's the same for ideas and information. You should never take someone else's ideas and information without giving them credit. That's what footnotes are for—to give people credit for their ideas.

HOW DO I WRITE THE RESEARCH PAPER?

Completing a research paper is like assembling a puzzle. This chapter will help you solve that puzzle. These ten steps will help you write a great research paper:

1. Make a list of research questions.

2. Read all about it—find books, magazines, and Internet information about your question.

3. Select a topic.

4. Write an outline.

5. Make a set of reference cards. These cards have information about the book, article, or other sources that you used.

6. Make a set of research cards. These cards have exact quotations from your research sources.

7. Construct a final outline based on the research cards.

8. Write a first draft of your paper based on the final outline.

9. Check the first draft. Be sure that you used the format your teacher required. Also, ask a parent or friend to read the paper so that you know that your ideas are easily understood by the reader.

10. Write a second draft.

STEP 1

Make a List of Research Questions

Research papers answer a question. You can't just write a paper "about dinosaurs." Instead, start with a question. For example, you might ask, "Why did the dinosaurs die?" or "What did the dinosaurs eat?" Make a list of questions now that you think are interesting. You don't have to write a research paper right now, but you will be happy to have a list like this when you do have to write a research paper:

I wish I knew the answer to these questions:

_____

_____

_____

_____

_____

STEP 2

Read All About It!

You will be surprised how much information there is on your research question. In fact, there is probably too much information. If you start out with a subject like "insects" or "dinosaurs," you will find thousands and thousands of pages of information. Visit the library and get to know your librarian. Librarians love books, and they are wonderful people. They like students who like to learn and have good questions. They will help you find things and save you lots of time. A word of warning: Everybody wants to see the librarian the day before a research paper is due. It would be a good idea if you became friends with the librarian long before your paper's due date. Research papers for fourth- and fifth-grade students require five to seven different books, articles, or Internet sources. If you can't find at least five research sources, then you may want to change your topic.

Choose a research question you find interesting, using the list of questions you wrote on page 85 or the list of questions at the end of this chapter. List some research sources that you would use to learn about that question.

My Research Question

_____

Research Sources

Books

_____

_____

_____

_____

_____

Magazine articles

_____

_____

_____

_____

_____

Internet sources

_____

_____

_____

_____

_____

Other research sources

_____

_____

_____

_____

_____

STEP 3

Select a Topic

Wait a minute. Didn't we already select the topic? Not really. You have a good research question, but that is not your final topic. What if you found too much information at the library? Then you might want to narrow your topic a little. What if you found too little information at the library? Then you definitely want to change your topic to something that has more information.

The topic for my research paper is

_____

Write an Outline

If you have never written an outline, let's take a minute to learn how to do it. Some teachers use Roman numerals (like I, II, and III for 1, 2, and 3). The Roman numerals are for the big ideas of your research paper. The letters are for the smaller ideas that are part of each big idea.

Here are two ideas for your outline. The "Big Idea" outline is a good model for a research paper that explains something. The "Alternative Answers" outline is a good model if you are asking a question that might have more than one answer and you want to help the reader understand which is the better answer.

"BIG IDEA" FOR RESEARCH PAPERS

I. Introduction
 A. Research question
 B. Reason the topic is interesting and important
 C. Very brief summary of the paper

II. Big Idea #1
 A. Tell the reader what the idea is
 B. Explain the idea
 C. Explain how the idea is a part of your research question

III. Big Idea #2
 A. Tell the reader what the idea is
 B. Explain the idea
 C. Explain how the idea is a part of your research question

IV. Big Idea #3
 A. Tell the reader what the idea is
 B. Explain the idea

C. Explain how the idea is a part of your research question

V. Conclusion
   A. Write the research question again
   B. Write the big ideas again
   C. Write your answer to research question
   D. Ask some more questions. What did you want to learn more about as a result of this research?

Figure 14.1 The "Big Idea" Outline for Research Papers

"ALTERNATIVE ANSWERS" OUTLINE FOR RESEARCH PAPERS

I. Introduction
   A. Research question
   B. Reason the topic is interesting and important
   C. Possible answers to the question

II. Possible Answer #1
   A. Identify the answer
   B. Explain the answer
   C. Evaluate the answer. Is it correct? Why?

III. Possible Answer #2
   A. Identify the answer
   B. Explain the answer
   C. Evaluate the answer. Is it correct? Why?

IV. Possible Answer #3
   A. Identify the answer
   B. Explain the answer
   C. Evaluate the answer. Is it correct? Why?

V. Conclusion
   A. Write the question again
   B. Write the possible answers to the question
   C. Write a conclusion. Which answer is correct?
   D. Ask some more questions. What did you want to learn more about as a
      result of this research?

Figure 14.2 "Alternative Answers" Outline for Research Papers

OUTLINE

(Please fill in your own labels, letters, and numbers)

Topic: _____

I. _____

   _____

   _____

   _____

II. _____

   _____

   _____

   _____

III. _____

_____

_____

_____

IV. _____

_____

_____

_____

V. _____

_____

_____

_____

_____

STEP 5

Make a Set of Reference Cards

Get some index cards. Sometimes your teacher will say exactly what size they should be. The big ones—5 inches tall and 8 inches wide—are the easiest ones to use. Make a separate card for each book, article, or other source that you have. If you use three different articles in the same issue of a magazine, make three different cards.

Research cards for books should answer the following questions:

1. What is the title? What is the subtitle?
2. What is the name of the author (or authors, if there are more than one)?
3. What is the name of the editor?
4. What city was it published in?
5. What is the name of the publisher?
6. What is the copyright date?
7. How many pages is it?

For magazines, you should write down the answers to these questions:

1. What is the full name of the author(s)?
2. What is the title of the article?
3. What is the full name of the magazine or journal?
4. What are the volume and issue numbers?
5. What are the page numbers on which the article appears?

For Internet information (which may include excerpts from books, magazines, newspapers, or other sources), you must include all the information listed above plus the complete Internet address. Some Internet addresses are long and confusing, but the reader of the research report must be able to trace any source you use. That is the reason that full source information is very important.

Bibliographic cards should look like this:

Walter, Martin S. "New Day Dawns in New York." *Monthly Magnet,* Vol. 32, no. 12, December 2001, pages 2–6.

Figure 14.3 Bibliographic Card: Magazine or Journal

Ellis, Dave. *Becoming a Master Student: Tools, techniques, hints, ideas, illustrations, examples, methods, procedures, processes, skills, resources, and suggestions for success.* Boston: Houghton Mifflin Company, 2001. 398 pages.

Figure 14.4 Bibliographic Card: Book

Haunshek, E. A. "Have We Learned Anything New? The RAND Study of NAEP Performance," *Education Matters More.* *www.edmattersmore.org/2001sp/haunshek.html.*
[Note: You must put the complete Internet address at the end of the title and journal information. The reason for this is that the reader must be able to find exactly the same information you used for your research paper.]

Figure 14.5 Bibliographic Card: Internet

STEP 6

Make a Set of Research Cards

Place direct quotations with important information from your sources on research cards. For example, the original source might contain this information from a research card:

BIRDS HURT BY OIL SPILLS [student caption of the research card]

Source: Edwards, Thomas J., "Migratory Birds in Peril," *Wildlife Alert* magazine, January 12, 1997, pages 13–14.

p. 13: "Oil spills kill thousands of migratory birds each year. Despite
cleanup efforts of shippers and oil companies, the damage is done too quickly
and the cleanup is too late for many birds whose feet and wings are soaked in
oil before rescuers can arrive."

Figure 14.6 Research Card

In most cases, you will have several research cards for each book or article that is used
as a source. Each research card should have only one important idea or piece of information.
If an article or book has many different ideas, facts, or conclusions that are interesting, each
separate idea should have its own research card. The top of the card should have a few
words that describe the main idea of the card. The rest of the card should contain the
source, the page number, and the exact quotation.

STEP 7

Write a Final Outline Based on the Research Cards

You're almost there. Because you did such a great job on the research, your first outline
must be expanded. For each part of the outline (look at the sections with letters—A, B, and
C), you now have much more information. Remember, writing a research paper is like solv-
ing a puzzle. Now you have all the pieces to the puzzle. Just like a puzzle, it helps to lay all
the research cards on a big table. Then put the cards that are similar all together so you can
see how the cards fit together. Sometimes they follow the outline perfectly. Other times,
you will need to add new parts to the outline because your research taught you new things

about the subject of your paper. For each letter, write some more details. When adding details under a letter, use numbers, like this:

I. Big Idea
    A. What is the big idea?
    B. Explain the big idea.
        1. Detail I learned in my research
        2. Another detail I learned in my research

Here is an example of a more detailed final outline.

FINAL OUTLINE

I. Introduction: We may know that dinosaurs all became extinct, but no one is sure why it happened.
    A. Why did the dinosaurs become extinct?
    B. It is important to think about why dinosaurs became extinct because it teaches us about our own world.

        1. Extinction might be necessary.
        2. Extinction might be avoidable.
        3. Dinosaur history can teach us valuable lessons.

    C. There are three main theories about how dinosaurs became extinct.

        1. There was a drastic change in the climate.
        2. An asteroid hit the earth.
        3. Food sources evolved too much.

II. Did a drastic change in the climate cause dinosaurs to become extinct?
    A. The climate suddenly became much colder.
    B. The climate change limited the dinosaurs' food supply.

        1. Dinosaurs needed water.
        2. Freezing temperatures made water harder to get to.

---

3. Freezing temperatures also caused plants and other food sources to die.

C. Could the climate change theory be the right one?

   1. Some evidence supports it.
   2. We still don't understand why the climate changed.
   3. The climate changes do not explain all of the dinosaur deaths.

III. Did the dinosaurs die because of an asteroid?
  A. An asteroid may have hit the earth.
  B. A single asteroid could cause a worldwide impact.

   1. There would have been huge changes in climate.
   2. The asteroid would have polluted the atmosphere.

C. Could the asteroid theory be the right one?

   1. There is evidence of asteroid craters.
   2. It would explain why large dinosaurs died in a short time period.
   3. It does not explain why some species survived.

IV. Did the evolution of food sources cause the dinosaurs' extinction?
  A. If food sources evolved, it would affect dinosaurs' diet.
  B. Changes in some species cause changes to other species.

   1. All species evolve, change, and die.
   2. When a food source changes or dies, other species may lose their food source.
   3. Compared to other species, dinosaurs lived a long time and were very successful.
   4. Changes take place over millions of years, not in a short period of time.

C. Could the food source theory be the right one?

   1. It is consistent with fossil evidence.
   2. It is also consistent with what we know of the dinosaurs' diet.
   3. Unfortunately, there is no clear evidence.

V. We must evaluate the possible theories of why the dinosaurs died.
  A. Why did the dinosaurs become extinct?
  B. The possible answers are a climate change, an asteroid, and a change
     in food supply.

  C. All three answers may be correct.
  D. There are other questions to research in the future.

    1. Do species still become extinct?
    2. What is happening to our food sources?
    3. Is the climate still changing?
    4. Do asteroids still hit the earth today?

Figure 14.7 Final Outline

STEP 8

Write a First Draft of Your Research Paper

Now you are ready to write your first draft. If your teacher provided directions, it is very important that you follow them. If your teacher provided a rubric or other information about how your research paper will be scored, then it is very important that you compare your work to the information provided by your teacher. If your teacher didn't give you any directions or information, then ask for some help. Every teacher I know is very happy when a student says, "Please tell me what I need to do to do a great job on this assignment."

STEP 9

Check the First Draft

Ask a parent or a friend to read your first draft. Does it make sense? Does it have some mistakes in spelling, punctuation, or grammar? Does it follow the teacher's directions?

Write a Second Draft

My students have a rule: Your first draft is never your last draft. We always write at least two drafts of every paper. That is how we show respect for the people who take the time to read our work, ask some questions, and make some suggestions. Sometimes we write more than two drafts. In fact, some students write five or six drafts before they are happy with their work and ready to give it to the teacher. When you are finished with your last draft, you will feel great. You wrote a real research paper! You worked very hard, and you deserve to celebrate. So take some time and think of your favorite thing to do, and do it! Show your parents your paper. Call your grandparents. Play a game. Eat some cookies. You deserve it!

The best topics for a research paper are the ones that you think of on your own. If you are having trouble thinking of topics, the box below offers some ideas.

Research Paper Starter Questions

Literature

- Charles Dickens wrote stories about how poor children lived in England. Did children really live that way?

- When Louisa May Alcott wrote *Little Women,* what was happening in American history?

- Why do some people want to see certain books banned?

- When Laura Ingalls Wilder wrote *Little House on the Prairie,* what was happening in American history?

- How does the life of an author affect the author's stories? (For example, how did the childhood of E. B. White, who wrote *Charlotte's Web* and *Trumpet of the Swan,* affect his stories?)

- Where did Shakespeare get his ideas for *Romeo and Juliet?*

- Where did Leonard Bernstein get his ideas for *West Side Story?*

- How does one of *Aesop's Fables* tell us something important today?

- What does Madeleine L'Engle's *A Wrinkle in Time* tell us about the family?

History

- What were the three main causes of the American Revolution?

- How was the town/city we live in first founded?

- How were women given the right to vote?

- What was the first organized government to give women the right to vote, and why?

- How did history influence the art of Norman Rockwell?

- How did history influence the music of the Baroque era?

- How has personal hygiene changed over the last three hundred years, and why?

- What were the main causes of the Civil War?

- Who were the greatest leaders of the Civil Rights movement, and how did their beliefs compare to each other?

Science

- How do astronauts train to survive in space?

- How did George Washington Carver's ideas help our society?

- How did Thomas Edison's inventions influence our society?

- How does the Black Plague of medieval times compare with modern diseases?

- What is the history of space travel?

- How does a compass work?

- How does a car engine work?

- How are stars used by sailors and pilots to help them find where they are?

- Why do some places have seasons, when others don't?

- Why were time zones invented?

- What is natural selection?

- How are dogs similar to and different from wolves?

- How do planes fly?

- What is the history of flight?

- What would you need to be able to survive on the planet Mars?

- How are humans and apes similar, and how are they different?

- How can we get energy from the sun?

- How do plants turn sunlight into food?

Geography

- What are plate tectonics, and how have they influenced the world's geography?

- How have African countries' names and borders changed over history?

- Why are English and French spoken in many places in Africa?

- How did the fall of the Iron Curtain affect Europe's geography?

- Why was Antarctica important in the 1800s and why is it important today?

- How did Lewis and Clark explore the Louisiana Purchase?

- Who, besides Christopher Columbus, discovered North America?

- How did the current Interstate Highway system come about?

Government

- What is the importance of the electoral college?

- How does the structure of the United States government compare with that of

Great Britain?

- What are the main responsibilities of the president of the United States?

- What officers are included in the president's cabinet, and what are their duties?

- What are the differences between a monarchy and a dictatorship?

- What did "the right to bear arms" mean when the Bill of Rights was written?

- What is parliamentary procedure, and how does it work?

- How did Social Security come into being?

- How does the system of "checks and balances" between the three branches of the U.S. government work, and why is it important?

Economics

- What is capitalism?

- What is socialism?

- How does capitalism compare to socialism?

- What caused the Great Depression?

- What do the words "Federal Reserve Note" on a one-dollar bill mean?

- What is a monopoly?

- What is an entrepreneur?

- How does supply and demand work?

15 The Genius Inside You:
Writing Stories, Poems, and Songs

ROBERT looked very unhappy as he threw a crumpled piece of notebook paper in the wastebasket. Just a minute ago he had seemed so happy as he finished his story. Now he was almost crying. I asked him what was wrong.

"Nobody got it," he said sadly. I bent over and took the paper out of the wastebasket and read the words. Robert was right. The words were hard to understand, and I couldn't figure out what he was trying to say. I took the paper, straightened out the crinkles, and sat down next to him.

"Tell me more about what this story is about," I said. "It looks like a great story, but you need to help me understand it."

Robert is a good writer with a good imagination. He knew all about the characters in his story. He dreamed about them. He made up funny voices for them. He drew pictures of them. But when he wrote his story, all the details stayed in Robert's head. He forgot to tell the reader all the information that he knew about his wonderful characters.

The best way to remember important details for your story is to use your senses—sight, touch, smell, feeling, and hearing. Now, think of a character that you might use in a story. Your character might be a child, an animal, an adult, or a creature from another planet. Think of any character you want, and then let's make that character come alive on the page. If you can't think of a character for a story yet, then write about a real person—yourself, a brother or sister, or a friend. You can even choose your family pet.

What is the character's name?

_____

Why is the character important in your story?

_____

_____

_____

What does the character look like?

_____

_____

_____

If you were really, really close to this character, what would the character smell like?

_____

_____

Touch the character's clothes or, if your character is an animal, touch the fur or skin or scales. What does it feel like?

_____

_____

When the character talks, how does it sound? Does your character's voice sound just like your voice or is it different?

_____

_____

ACTION! WHAT DOES YOUR CHARACTER DO?

Now that you know what your character looks like, let's think about what the character will do. Describe everything this character will do in your story.

Before my story started, this character was:

_____

_____

_____

At the beginning of the story, this character:

_____

_____

_____

Then, all of a sudden, this character:

_____

_____

_____

Finally, this character:

_____

_____

_____

For each character in your story, write a detailed description based on the sights, sounds, smells, and feel of that character. Then write a plan for what each character is going to do in the story. Now, you are ready to write your first draft. Good stories have a clear beginning, middle, and end. Start your story with a few words that grab the reader's attention. This will make your reader want to read more. You can use your own experience to start a story and then add your creative energy to make a fantastic story. Here is one example of a story that grabs the reader's attention right away.

> *Henry Higgenbothem had just gotten his third bloody nose this week. As usual, he ran to his room and hugged his dog, Samson, and lay on the bed crying. What happened next was not usual at all. "You had a bad day?" asked Samson. "Wha—wha—what did you say?" stammered Henry. He had never heard a dog speak before. Samson licked Henry's face and replied, "I asked if you had a bad day. We can't let this problem with Billy the Bully continue, so let's put our heads together and find a solution." Henry was too surprised to speak, so he listened as Samson provided a plan for the next day.*

Now you try it. You know your character and you have planned your story. Write an opening paragraph that will grab the reader's attention.

Great job! Now, finish the first draft of your story. Remember to help the reader picture and understand the characters and action in your story. When you are finished, ask a parent or friend to read your story, ask questions, and make suggestions.

```
┌─────────────────────────────────────────────────────────┐
│                                                           │
│     _____     │
│                                                           │
│     _____     │
│                                                           │
│     _____     │
│                                                           │
│     _____     │
│                                                           │
│     _____     │
│                                                           │
└─────────────────────────────────────────────────────────┘
```

 POETRY

Writing poetry is a great way to relax and have fun. Poetry can be described as a dance of words. You can play with sounds, rhythms, and meanings so that you create a wonderful picture for the reader with only a few words. Many types of poetry have a structure, and within that structure you can create a lot of different sounds, rhythms, and feelings.

Let's start with a word poem in which each letter of the word begins a line of the poem. The lines do not have to rhyme. For example, you might choose to write a poem to your mother in which each line begins with the letters M-O-T-H-E-R. You could write a poem about soccer in which each line begins with the letters S-O-C-C-E-R. Choose a word that has meaning for you and write your word poem in the space below. Put the first word of each letter along the left-hand side of the page, and then complete your poem:

Title: _____

_____

_____

_____

_____

_____

_____

_____

_____

That was great! Now let's try a different type of poetry.

Haiku

Haiku is a form of poetry developed by the Japanese. The poem is only three lines long. The rules for haiku are based on the number of syllables in the line. A syllable is a single sound in a word. For example, the word *song* has one syllable, and the word *singing* has two syllables. *Goldilocks* has three syllables. In haiku, the first line consists of five syllables, the second of seven, and the third of five.

For example:

Poems make words sing [*five syllables*]
Poems make words come alive [*seven syllables*]
Poems make me smile [*five syllables*].

Now you try it.

[five syllables] _____

[seven syllables] _____

[five syllables] _____

Good job! Now let's try some other forms of poetry. Did you know that the words of songs are a type of poetry? Think of a song that you already know, and then write your own poem that goes with that music. Here is an example to help you get started. We could start with the song "My Country 'Tis of Thee."

The real words of the song begin like this:

My country 'tis of thee
Sweet land of liberty
Of thee I sing.

Did you notice that the first two lines rhyme? We could take the same pattern of rhythm and sounds to make our own poem. We might begin:

My life is sweet today
I'll go outside and play
And make a mess.

Now you try it. You can use any song you want, but you should use a song that you know so well that you can hear it in your head.

Write the words of the song on the left side of the page, and then write your new poem on the right side of the page. Remember to use exactly the same rhythm and rhyme so that you could sing your poem to the tune of the song.

There are many other types of poems, and not all of them have strict rules for rhyme and rhythm. As a poet, you can write what you feel using words and sounds to help the reader understand your feelings in a way that is more personal and special than if you were talking or writing a paragraph. Sometimes your words will rhyme, and other times they won't—it's up to you. The most important thing is that your poem uses the right words in exactly the right way to express how you feel. You have already written poems that follow strict rules. Now try writing a poem with no rules at all. Just write about something that you feel deeply about.

16 My Parents and Teachers Don't Understand Me! Talking About Your Writing with Adults

You know your parents love you. You know your teachers care about you. But most kids still get frustrated with their parents and teachers sometimes. Guess what? I'll bet that your parents were frustrated with their parents sometimes, too. Your teachers were frustrated with their teachers. It just happens. In this chapter, we'll learn about how to talk about your writing with adults. You will learn when to ask for help and when to work on your own.

First, think about what the meanest parents in the world might say about your writing. Imagine showing one of your poems in the last chapter to the meanest parents in the world. What would they say?

Now, what would the nicest parents in the world say about your poem?

```
_____

_____

_____

_____

_____
```

Most kids think that the mean parents would say that the poem is terrible and that nice parents would say that the poem is wonderful. But when you think about it, what writers really need is for parents to be kind, gentle, truthful, and helpful. How much help would it be if your parents always said, "Every word is perfect!" How would you ever become a better writer? Parents and teachers who are kind, gentle, truthful, and helpful want to tell us how great our writing is, and they also want to tell us how we can write even better.

You can help your parents help you become the best writer you can be. Put the following four ideas into your own words and share these thoughts with them the next time you talk about your writing.

Please don't tell me it's perfect.

I know you love me, but the best way to help is to ask me questions about my writing and make suggestions for making it better. I admit that sometimes I'd like you to say that everything is perfect and nothing has to be changed, but we both know that probably isn't true. So it's okay to tell me my writing isn't perfect. I already knew that!

Please don't tell me everything that is wrong with it.

Yes, I know I just said that I want you to make some suggestions, but give me a break! I really work on my writing, and I'm very proud of it. I'll get discouraged if you tell me that too many things are wrong. I know I'm going to make several drafts. I'll probably think of things I want to change even if you don't make suggestions. Please give me three or four ideas for improvement. If you do any more than that or if you make marks on every single line, I will get frustrated.

Read my teacher's guidelines for writing.

Some teachers call this a rubric. Other teachers call it a scoring guide. Other teachers just have a set of rules. Whatever they call it, please read it. It may not be the same set of rules you had when you were a kid, and I really want to follow my teacher's rules. If my teacher hasn't provided any guidelines (or if I can't find them) then it's okay if you ask my teacher for them. Most teachers are really happy when parents take an interest in their children's work.

Never give up on me.

I get discouraged sometimes—everybody does. Because you love me so much and don't want to see me upset, you might want to say something like, "It's okay—you're doing the best you can," and let me turn in work that we both know isn't as good as it should be. Even if I get a little frustrated with you, don't give up and don't let me off the hook. Even though I may not say it at the time, I really want to do my best work, and I like it when you challenge me.

Now, take a minute and write your own list for your parents.

Please help me be the best writer I can be. Here are some ways you can help:

_____

_____

_____

_____

_____

_____

_____

_____

_____

TALKING WITH YOUR TEACHER

I work with teachers all over the world. They are such great people! They love kids. They work hard. They really care about you, not just as a student, but also as a person. Sometimes teachers get frustrated, just as you do. When I hear kids say that a teacher is mean or mad, it usually means the teacher is frustrated. Teachers want to do a good job, just like you do, but sometimes it isn't easy. If you and your teacher get frustrated, here are some things you can do to improve your writing and also improve how you and your teacher get along.

Ask questions.

It takes courage to ask for help. Often teachers ask, "Does anyone have any questions?" and everyone is quiet. But often kids _do_ have questions—lots of them. They are just afraid to be the only one to ask. If kids don't ask questions and an assignment isn't clear, the teacher and the students will get frustrated. The number-one rule of being a good student is to ask questions.

Practice grading your own work.

Your teacher probably has a scoring guide, or a rubric. If your teacher has not given you a copy of the scoring guide, ask for one. Try saying something like, "I'd like to try to grade my own writing before I hand it in. Would that be okay?" Every teacher I know would be very happy to hear a student say those words. When you practice grading your own writing, it is important to look at your work in the same way your teacher does. The teacher doesn't know what you meant to write, only what you actually wrote down on the paper. You will help yourself the most if you try to see your paper the way your teacher would.

Ask for samples of great student work.

One of the best ways to learn more about writing is to read the work of other writers. Of course, you should always be reading books that you love and books that your teacher tells you to read. You should also read stories and essays written by other students. Some teachers keep examples of student writing from last year or even many years ago. Tell your teacher that you would like to see lots of examples of great student writing. Knowing what great student writing looks like will help you become a better writer.

Always correct your work.

Many students don't understand why it is so important to correct their work. They write an essay or a story, give it to the teacher, and then the teacher makes some corrections and gives it back. When I ask the students to make corrections and rewrite their story or essay, they sometimes say, "But I already did it! The teacher already graded it! Why should I do it again?" At the Stanley School newspaper, where I help elementary students write lots of stories, we have a rule. The rule is, "Your first draft is never your last draft." Every student—even the very best writers in the school—always have a conference with another student and sometimes with a parent or teacher. They get ideas, make corrections, and write another draft. That should be your rule as well. Even if your teacher has already given you a grade, make it a habit to always correct your work and write the best story or essay that you can. Your teacher might be surprised if you rewrite something even when you don't have to. But your teacher will be happy that you are working so hard on your writing. Remember, you are not just writing for your teacher. You are writing for you, and you will be much happier when you know that you are doing your very best work.

17 Now It's Really Important:
Writing for State Tests

EVERY state tests students in reading and math. More and more states also have a writing test. Some states have writing tests that ask students to write stories. Other states ask students to write about science. Some states ask students to write about a personal experience, and other states ask students to write about an event in history.

Even though states have different tests, here are some things that every state requires.

YOU MUST WRITE NEATLY

If you have heard people say that you don't need to make your letters neat because you can just use a computer, they are wrong. Everybody—students, teachers, and parents—needs to be able to write using a pencil or pen so that other people understand what is written. On state tests, it doesn't matter whether you print or write in cursive, but you must write neatly.

YOU MUST BE ORGANIZED

Everything you write, whether it is a story or an essay, must have a clear beginning, middle, and end. You have already learned that a graphic organizer or an outline can help you organize your writing. Some states encourage students to do "pre-writing" activities, including the creation of an outline or organizer. Other states just give students a question and expect them to start writing. No state—not a single one—has outlawed the use of outlines and organizers. So, even if your state test does not require an outline or give you time for it, do it anyway! Scratch paper is always available, or you can just use the last page of the paper provided for your essay to create an outline or organizer. This will save you time and allow you to write a much better essay.

YOU MUST WRITE A LOT

How much is "a lot"? If you are in the first or second grade, you should plan to write five to seven sentences in one paragraph for any state test. If you are in third or fourth grade, you should write three paragraphs, each paragraph having about five sentences. If you are in fifth grade, then you should write five paragraphs, each paragraph having about five sentences. Your opening and closing paragraphs can be a little shorter, with three or four sentences.

One of the hardest things about writing for state tests is that you don't have your teacher, parents, or friends to help you review your work. You are on your own. When you review your own work, remember the code word QUIET. Each letter stands for a step that will help you review your work.

Q—Question: Did I answer the question in the test?

U—Understand: Can I understand what I just wrote? Are the letters neat and the ideas clear?

I—Interest: Is it interesting, with great details and examples?

E—Errors: Did I check for correct spelling, capitalization, punctuation, and grammar?

T—Topic: Does the first sentence tell about the rest of the essay? Does that lead to a clear beginning, middle, and end?

WHAT IF YOU GET WORRIED ABOUT TESTS?

If you are worried about state tests, some people might try to tell you, "Hey—those tests are no big deal—just don't worry about it!" But if you are really worried, that doesn't help you very much. Think about your favorite doctor or dentist. You might have been worried when you went to his or her office, but the best doctors and dentists don't just take out a machine and start working on you. They stop, talk with you, and help you understand what they are going to do and why they are going to do it. They don't say, "Don't worry about it." They don't lie to you. They will say, "This is going to pinch," or "This might sting, but it's just going to be for a second." They will also help you understand why they are doing things and how they are helping you get better. If you are upset and concerned about a test, it doesn't do any good for me to say, "Don't worry about it." So let's talk about what to do when you are worried about an important state test.

The best way to reduce your fear about any test is to learn more about the test. Most states give teachers and parents sample questions. These sample questions can help you know what to expect on the test. If your teacher has not already given you some sample questions, ask for some. Information about the test is also available on your state department of education's Web site. Some state Web sites have sample questions, and many even have sample student essays. You might be worried that looking at questions before the test is cheating. That is not true. Cheating is when you sneak into the state department of education office, peek at the real test questions, and then practice answers just for those questions. I don't think you are going to do that! It is not cheating when you learn what the test questions are like, how the state will score your test, and what you need to study in order to do your very best work.

Practice writing essays in a way that is similar to the way you will take the test. For example, if you will have to sit still and write for forty-five minutes without talking to anyone or asking a teacher or parent for help during the state test, you should practice doing just that. For a full forty-five minutes, don't answer the phone, watch television, or ask for help. Just work on a sample essay, such as the ones listed below.

Think like a test maker. If you were going to grade student tests for your state, what would be important to you? You would need to be able to read the tests, so they would have to be written neatly. You would find it easier to read essays that were well organized. And you would expect each student to write enough to cover the subject. If a student only wrote a few sentences, you probably would not like the essay very much.

Let's try it. Here are five questions that are similar to questions on recent state tests. Pick one and write about it. First, complete a graphic organizer or outline. Then write a first draft. Review and make corrections to your first draft, and then write your final draft.

- Think of a person who has been an important influence in your life. Write an essay that will help the reader understand why that person is so important to you and what that person means to you today.

- Some schools have uniforms and others don't. What do you think? Are school uniforms a good idea? Write an editorial for your local newspaper that explains your point of view.

- Think of a person in history who is no longer living. Write an essay that explains who this person was and why this person was important.

- Write a letter to the principal of your school. The purpose of your letter is to persuade the principal to make a decision on something that is important to you. You may choose any topic you wish for your letter.

- Think of a game that you like to play. Write an essay explaining how to play that game. The person reading your essay has never played the game before, so you must explain every part of the game as carefully and as clearly as you can.

Outline or Graphic Organizer

_____

_____

_____

_____

_____

_____

_____

_____

_____

_____

_____

_____

_____

_____

_____

_____

_____

_____

_____

_____

_____

_____

First Draft

Final Draft

_____

_____

_____

_____

_____

_____

_____

_____

_____

_____

_____

_____

_____

_____

_____

_____

_____

_____

_____

_____

_____

_____

18 Developing the Habit of Writing

TAKE a minute and look at all the writing you have done so far in this workbook. You started by writing just a few sentences about yourself. Then you wrote paragraphs, poems, letters, and essays. You are a writer! Now that you have worked so hard, it is important that you keep the habit of writing alive. Here are some ideas that you and your parents can use to make writing a habit. Writing is not just a skill for school; it is a skill for life. Many years from now, you will be writing in college, in a job, or just for fun. If writing becomes a habit for you, the writing that you do in the future will be fun and rewarding.

Now that you have looked at your writing, pick two or three pieces that you like the best. Write the titles here and write a few words about why this is your best work.

My Best Writing

Title _____

This is some of my best work because:

_____

_____

_____

_____

Title _____

This is some of my best work because:

_____

_____

_____

_____

_____

Title _____

This is some of my best work because:

_____

_____

_____

_____

_____

Now that you have thought about your best work, you probably want to do more writing just like that. Here are five things that you can do to keep up the habit of writing:

MAKE A PLACE FOR YOUR SPECIAL WRITING SUPPLIES

I'm not talking about the notebook paper and pencils that you have to share with the whole family. I mean special paper and special pencils and pens that you have picked out just for your writing. The next time you have a birthday or other special day and people ask what you would like as a gift, you can tell them that you would like special paper, pens, and pencils for your personal writing supply. Each of my children has a special kind of paper for writing. Julia likes colored paper. Brooks likes heavy white paper. Jamie likes paper with borders on it.

START A DIARY OR A JOURNAL

This is personal. Nobody gets to read it except you. You can write your ideas, the events of your day, and the things that make you happy, sad, or mad. If you take just a few minutes at the end of each day to write in your journal, you will begin a lifelong habit of writing. When you read your journal entries weeks, months, and years from now, you will be surprised at what you have written. You will remember deep feelings and funny events. When you write in a journal, it is as if you are talking to a trusted friend who will always keep your secrets.

MAKE SOME PERSONALIZED STATIONERY

You can do this on a computer or with a rubber stamp set. Some stationery has a name on the top, and other people put their name, address, and phone number. It's your stationery, so you can do whatever you want. You can also put decorations, symbols, initials, or anything else you want. When you send letters using your personalized stationery, the people who receive your letters will know that the letters are from you before they see your name on the envelope. This will make writing letters fun. Of course, the more letters you write, the more letters you will receive.

WRITE NOTES TO YOUR PARENTS AND FRIENDS

Would you like to know how to make your mom or dad happy and surprised? Write a note and secretly put it in their briefcase, purse, lunch box, or some other place where they will find it during the day. It doesn't have to be a long letter. Just a few sentences will make them feel happy and proud of you. If you have a friend who is having a tough day, try writing a short note to cheer him up. It will make you feel great to know that you did something nice for someone else. Who knows? You might even get some notes in your lunch box.

DISPLAY YOUR WRITING

Some families put school papers on the refrigerator door, and other families have bulletin boards. You probably have some space on the wall in a bedroom or other place in the house. Use that space to show the writing that you especially like. When you see your very best writing on the wall, each time you look at it you will remind yourself that you are a great writer!

19 Your Writer's Tool Kit

WRITERS need more than paper, pencils, and pens. They need tools to help them work with words and ideas. Here are some tools that you can use to help you in every writing project.

Every writer needs a dictionary. The dictionary helps you spell words correctly and understand the meanings of words. It will also help you choose just the right word for your own writing. If something is very good, is it wonderful, fantastic, great, or fabulous? Are all of these words the same? Or are there small differences that a writer should consider?

Another useful tool is the thesaurus. This book will help you find words that have similar meanings. These words are called synonyms. For example, in the last paragraph, *wonderful, fantastic, great,* and *fabulous* are all synonyms. Now you try it. Think of all the words you can think of that are synonyms for the word *bad* and list them below:

Synonyms for the word *bad*

_____

_____

_____

_____

_____

How many words did you think of? When you are writing about an idea, event, person, or place that is bad, you can describe it in many different ways. Here are some words you might use:

Bad:
Awful
Terrible
Dreadful
Appalling
Ghastly
Unpleasant
Odious

You probably already know some of these words. Others (such as "odious") are probably new to you. When you use a thesaurus, you can build your vocabulary very quickly because you learn words in clusters. Each time you use the thesaurus, you learn words that mean very close to the same thing, and now you know several new ways to say that something is bad!

Another useful tool for writers is an almanac. This book is full of facts about almost everything in the world. There are facts about animals, governments, people, climates, and many other things. Ask your school librarian for an almanac and look at the table of contents. It's amazing! You can find the answers to many different questions. As a writer, you can find examples, statistics, and facts to support your writing. Although you would never want to use the almanac as the only reference for a paper in school, it is an excellent place to start.

If you enjoy writing poetry, you might find a rhyming dictionary useful. You learned that some poetry rhymes and other poetry does not. If you are working on a poem that has rules for rhymes, then a rhyming dictionary will help you find words that you might not think of on your own.

Each year, more and more kids use the Internet. It's a great tool, but it also has some strange and dangerous features. It's like going to a hardware store. In one section there are interesting tools, pipes, and paints. Then you turn the corner and right in front of you is a saw blade so sharp it could cut off your finger! On the Internet, you could be searching for something and suddenly find words, pictures, and people that are not appropriate. Even some of the Web sites that say that they will help kids become better writers do not have good supervision, and some of them are not very good. If you want to use the Internet for research or to share your writing with other students, be sure to do so with a parent's supervision.

APPENDIX A
Checking Your Own Writing

It is always best to use the scoring guide that your teacher prefers. If your teacher doesn't have one available, then you can use this checklist to review your own writing projects.

☑ I answered the question or did exactly what the writing prompt asked me to do.

☑ I know who my audience is, and I am writing directly to that audience.

☑ I have a strong first sentence that tells the reader what to expect.

☑ I have a clear beginning, middle, and end.

☑ I support my ideas with lots of details and examples.

☑ My descriptions use rich, colorful language.

☑ When I start a new idea, I start a new paragraph.

☑ Each paragraph is indented.

☑ Every sentence begins with a capital letter, and the names of people and places also begin with capital letters.

☑ Every sentence ends with correct punctuation — a period, exclamation point, or question mark.

☑ The words are spelled correctly.

☑ When I read it aloud, it sounds right — I'm pretty sure that there are no errors in grammar.